Britain's Hot Potato!

a boiled-down guide to the European Union, the constitution debate, the euro, and us

A.M. Crosbie

HBI PUBLISHING
(www.hot-potato.info)

This edition published in Great Britain in 2004 by
HBI Publishing
28 Dursley Road
Heywood
Wiltshire
BA13 4LG

A catalogue record for this book is available
from the British Library

ISBN: 0-9547723-0-X

Cover design by The Bath Design Centre
Printed and bound in England by Cox & Wyman of Reading

Britain's Hot Potato!

A boiled-down guide to the European Union, the constitution debate, the euro, and us

Containing everything you need to know
about the European Union:

- history
- eu budgets
- the single currency
- eu inflation
- basic economics
- the uk euro debate
- the constitution debate
- trivia
- progress check-lists
- glossary

- enlargement
- eu voting
- european central bank
- stability & growth pact
- economic reform
- federalism
- 'info stops'
- statistics
- further resources
- quiz

You will never find such a painless means of gathering impartial information about Europe!

"*a note from the author;*
This book is impartial - after four years of researching the European Union even I can't decide what I really think of it! I have, however, included the odd expression of incredulity or sarcasm. Please don't read any political bias into these flippant comments. More often than not, I'm just expressing my genuine astonishment. By the way, I offer no guarantee that you will form your own opinion by the end of this book. But I do guarantee you'll be astonished! **"**

ONCE UPON A TIME!

The beginnings of the European Union - or the 'EU' as it's often called - hark back to 1951 and a little agreement called the Treaty of Paris. The Treaty was between six countries - Belgium, France, Germany, Italy, Luxembourg and the Netherlands - and established The European Coal & Steel Community.

You see, according to the 'official history,' the beginnings of the European Union evolved from concern that the production of coal and steel should be pooled, and its consumption collectively managed, as a part of the post-war unification of Europe.

TO BE MORE EXPLICIT

After World War Two, Germany's neighbours - France especially - were a bit nervous that Germany's economic and political rebuilding might provide them with new capabilities to wage war. The European Coal and Steel Community was suggested by the French Government, because the pooling of steel and coal resources would, they said, make war between France and Germany 'materially impossible.' Additionally, economic co-operation between nation states was seen as a means to prevent political conflict of a scale witnessed in World War Two. (Which, so far - touch wood and all that - it has.)

TIME TO UNITE

Prior to the Treaty of Paris, world events had already been focusing the minds of Europe's leaders on the importance of trust and co-operation. Firstly, the U.S. Secretary of State, General Marshall, offered significant financial aid to post-war Europe, on the condition that European Governments 'co-ordinate their needs and act jointly in allocating the aid.'

Then, the Russians declined General Marshall's offer of financial assistance and its conditional co-operation. The Cold War began, and a new political divide went up across Europe.

In 1948 the Russians put up their Berlin blockade. In the same year Czechoslovakia suffered its Communist coup. Then in 1950 the Korean War broke out, and the Western world discovered the North Koreans had been fully armed by the Russians. With this, the integration of post-war Germany into a 'new Europe' became even more critical to ensuring lasting peace on the continent.

NB. Later in the book we will discuss the ideas for a 'Federal United Europe' that evolved in the 1920s. Some people suggest that the end of World War Two and the start of the Cold War make a convenient starting point for the 'official history' of the European Union, and that the role of federalism is played down because it is politically beneficial to do so.

WARNING. Contradictory opinions exist on almost everything relating to the European Union (including its historical development)!

THE TREATY OF ROME

The Treaty of Paris worked very well, and calls soon came for the alliance to be expanded upon. In 1957 the Treaty of Rome established the European Economic Community (EEC).

The EEC also became known as the Common Market. Put simply, its aims were:
▸ To free up the movement of goods between participating countries, unimpeded by customs duties and other restrictions.
▸ To free up the movement of labour, services, and capital.
▸ To establish trade protection for participating countries, by establishing a common external tariff on goods imported from countries outside of the European Economic Community.

A second Treaty of Rome established the European Atomic Energy Community (Euratom), which promoted research and development in the field of atomic energy, and ensured the peaceful and appropriate use of nuclear energy.

So, three European Communities were established in the 1950s:
▸ The European Coal and Steel Community
▸ The European Economic Community
▸ The European Atomic Energy Community.

In 1965 a Merger Treaty created a Single Commission and Single Council for the Communities. The EEC was to become the most significant and well known of the three.

EU TREATIES

A treaty is an agreement between different governments. The rules that govern the modern European Union have evolved via a number of treaties over the years. Each treaty makes new 'rules' governing how the European Union works, and outlines new or altered powers.

1951 **Paris:** (dates given are those of treaty signing)
Established the European Coal and Steel Community.

1957 **Rome:**
Two treaties established the European Economic Community and the European Atomic Energy Community.
1965: A Merger Treaty created a Single Commission and Single Council for the three European Communities.
1985: The Single European Act significantly revised the Treaty of Rome. It committed the European Community to the concept of a 'single market.'

1992 **Maastricht:**
'The Treaty on European Union' did several things. The European Economic Community was renamed the European Community, which became one area - or 'pillar' - of a new structure called the European Union. Two new 'pillars' were added: The Common Foreign and Security Policy (foreign affairs), and co-operation in Justice and Home Affairs (criminal law).

1997 **Amsterdam:**
Significantly amended the Treaties of Rome and Maastricht.

2001 **Nice:**
Merged key former treaties into one new version, preparing the EU for expansion.

(NB. A new **Constitutional Treaty** is due soon ...)

WHAT ABOUT THE UK?

The UK didn't join the first European Community - The European Coal and Steel Community - because at the time it was formed in 1951 the government had just nationalised our coal and steel industries (with some difficulty and amidst immense controversy).* The UK did send a representative to the initial Treaty of Rome negotiations, but withdrew (thinking nothing would come of the negotiations anyway).

When the Treaty of Rome was actually ratified, the folk in Westminster were somewhat concerned. They went off and formed the European Free Trade Area (EFTA) in 1960, with six other European countries that hadn't signed the Treaty of Rome. Importantly, the European Free Trade Area excluded agriculture, and didn't have the same ambitions for political and economic integration as the European Economic Community. This is important because Westminster hoped the European Free Trade Area might be merged with the European Economic Community (and thus the UK would regain some influence). But agriculture was an important element of the Common Market, and the European Economic Community members (France especially) weren't interested in a merger of any kind, at the time.**

For more background to the UK's decision see page 77.
**Many decades later, in 1994, a merger did occur, which created the European Economic Area. Switzerland was the only EFTA member not to join, after the Swiss public voted no to the idea in a referendum.*

A PROSPEROUS COMMUNITY

Between 1958 and 1972 the economies of the European Economic Community's six member countries grew faster than the world's richest country, the U.S.A. In 1958 the UK was more prosperous than all six member countries of the European Economic Community, but by 1972 had been overtaken by all of them except Italy.

THE FRENCH VETO OUR JOINING

By the early 1960's the UK had realised the dangers of being isolated from the European Economic Community, so it applied to join. But in 1963 the French President, General de Gaulle, used his veto to block their entry. (Ireland and Denmark were also applying to join, and both countries withdrew their applications in protest.) In 1967 the UK again applied to join. And again President de Gaulle used his veto to prevent it. The other members of the European Economic Community, as well as many of the French public, didn't entirely agree with de Gaulle's actions. Luckily for the UK, in 1969 he resigned.

A European Economic Community Summit in December 1969 was attended by the new French President, Pompidou. The Summit agreed to open negotiations for the UK's entry.

JRE ABOUT de GAULLE

To justify his veto, President De Gaulle commented that Britain was not yet 'sufficiently European in outlook' and too tied to the USA. In fact, it seems it was the Common Agriculture Policy that kept the UK out of the EEC in the 1960s. You see, in the 1950s the French Government had substantially increased agricultural subsidies (because it was politically expedient to do so.) President de Gaulle acknowledged that France couldn't afford such farming subsidies. France needed new export markets for the surplus produce the subsidies were creating, and a new source of funding to pay for the subsidies. De Gaulle realised that the European Economic Community could provide the solution!

De Gaulle also realised that the UK would oppose its proposal for a Common Agricultural Policy - which would raise levies on imported goods as a means of generating income. (The UK imported huge amounts of agricultural goods from its Commonwealth - in 1961 over 50% of New Zealand's exports came to the UK.) De Gaulle needed to stall the UK's entry until after the details of the CAP had been agreed, for once they were in place it would be difficult for the UK alone to change them. Edward Heath made this comment in his memoirs:

'The French did not wish the British to be at the table taking part in the formative discussions on the CAP, for fear that we might disrupt the very favourable arrangements they otherwise had every reason to expect from the partners.'

THE COMMON MARKET

Meanwhile, although economies in the European Economic Community were growing, concerns remained about the effectiveness of the Common Market. Despite the Customs Union that was created in 1968 (which abolished all customs duties on trade between member countries), significant barriers to achieving the objectives of the Common Market remained. Notably:

▸ Technical barriers, e.g., differences in technical or professional standards
▸ Differences in national government policies regarding excise and VAT
▸ Resident and work permit issues.

These issues remained a problem for the next two decades. Eventually, in 1987, The Single European Act came into effect. The Single European Act outlined ways to address the barriers (physical, technical and fiscal) that still impeded the free movement of goods, people and investment between participating countries. It proposed many changes to the European Economic Community, but the most relevant are:

▸ The concept of the Single Market was developed (to replace the Common Market).

▸ Economic and Monetary Union (EMU) became a key objective of The Single Market.

THE MAASTRICHT TREATY

It took a few years to sort out the fine print of the Single European Act. Its aims were embodied in The Maastricht Treaty, which was signed, finally, in 1992. The Maastricht Treaty changed many aspects of the former two European Treaties, and embodied the Single Market and Economic and Monetary Union as a cornerstone for the future. Also, the European Economic Community became the European Community. The European Community became one of three 'pillars' of a new structure, called the European Union.

DOUBTS ABOUT THE UNION

Ratification of The Maastricht Treaty was a long and arduous process. First, in 1992 the Danish electorate rejected ratification of the Treaty in a closely contested referendum (50.7% against and 49.3% for). The Irish meanwhile voted 69% for and 31% against, whilst the French mustered only a nail-biting 51.05% support. In May 1992 a second Danish referendum ratified the Treaty with 58.6% support.

If you can't remember voting in the UK's Maastricht Treaty referendum, its because there wasn't one! John Major's Government awaited a positive Danish referendum before putting a Bill through Parliament as a means of ratifying the treaty. (A few people weren't very happy about this.)

WHAT IS THE EU?

The five key objectives of the European Union are:

▶ To promote economic and social progress
▶ To assert the European Union's identity on the international scene
▶ To introduce European citizenship
▶ To develop an area of 'freedom, security and justice'
▶ To maintain and build on established European Union law.

The European Union has five institutions. They are:

▶ **European Parliament** = members are elected democratically by the citizens of member states, every five years.

▶ **European Council** = represents the Governments of member states. Members states take it in turns to 'preside' over the Council. It is where the most important decision-making takes place. Leaders of member states meet twice a year at a Summit Meeting. There are also over 20 committees of the Council (e.g. Finance, Agriculture, Transport), comprised of relevant Ministers from member state governments.

▶ **European Commission** = the executive body of the European Commission: the place from which the civil servants issue all the legislation and directives.

▶ **Court of Justice** = does legal stuff.
▶ **Court of Auditors** = does auditing stuff.

WHAT DOES THE EU DO?

In its earlier vestiges, the European Union concentrated on trade and economic issues. Today it covers a wide range of issues and activities, relating to areas such as:

Citizens' Rights	Justice
Job Creation	Regional Development
Environmental Protection	Education & Training
Transport	Research & Innovation
Public Health	Humanitarian Aid
Fraud	Food Safety
Energy	Agriculture & Fisheries
The Information Society	Customs
Asylum & Immigration	Peace keeping.

The European Union does many things. Here are some examples. The EU:

▶ gives out grants of various kinds
▶ gives subsidies to farmers and other primary sector industries
▶ runs Pilots Schemes and carries out research
▶ funds regional development in the poorer parts of Europe
▶ issues a vast amount of new rules and directives to make improvements to relevant sectors
▶ gives aid to the developing world
▶ makes laws and monitors laws
▶ makes Europe-wide policies on things such as pollution
▶ collects public opinion and data, and issues statistics
▶ lends money for large infrastructure projects (through the European Investment Bank)
▶ promotes Europe-wide economic reforms
▶ undertakes peace-keeping actions in various parts of the world.

WHAT HAS THE EU ACHIEVED?

Here is a completely random list of examples. The EU has:

▶ Made us put catalytic converters in our cars, and got rid of leaded petrol.

▶ Helped UK educational and professional qualifications be recognised throughout the EU.

▶ Improved the quality of our beaches (through water pollution directives).

▶ Promoted economic growth and funded large-scale infrastructure projects in the EU's poorer regions (via its 'Structural Funds' and the European Investment Bank.)

▶ The 5th Enlargement will improve the standard of living in ten Central and Eastern European Countries.

▶ Helped to double the number of households with internet access between 2000 and 2003, via the 'eEurope' project.

▶ Agreed to limit catches of cod, hake and plaice for the next ten years (which is the first time such a 'long term recovery programme' has been agreed - putting ecology before economies).

▶ Enabled EU citizens to access hospitals and doctors in any member state they are travelling in (get form E111 from the Post Office!)

▶ Funded the planting of circa. 1,000,000 hectares of new forest.

▶ Fined one group of firms, in 1994, over 248 million 'Ecus' for price-fixing and market rigging.

▶ Fined Microsoft US$613 million for using its Windows monopoly to stifle competition.

▶ Signed, in 2003, the 'Framework Convention on Combating Tobacco' which included a ban on tobacco advertising and the requirement for clearer health warnings on tobacco packaging.

▶ Established new common rules on compensation and passenger rights in the event of denied boarding, cancellation or long delays of air flights.

WHAT HAS THE EU ACHIEVED?

Here's another random list. The EU has:

▶ Established a directive ordering compulsory labelling on foodstuffs produced with genetically modified ingredients.

▶ To date contributed €1.6 billion to the Debt Alleviation Initiative (established in 1999 by the World Bank) to reduce the debt of highly-indebted developing countries.

▶ Launched (literally!) the Galileo Satellite Radio-Navigation System, in partnership with the European Space Agency.

▶ Introduced rules to limit the travelling times for the transportation of live animals.

▶ Launched, in 2003, a 5-year, €351m research and development programme to help combat HIV/Aids, malaria and tuberculosis in developing countries.

▶ Introduced legislation to harmonise bank charges for electronic transfers and cash machine withdrawals across the EU.

▶ Made driver training obligatory for drivers of certain vehicles, e.g. passenger coaches.

▶ Established the AGIS Programme to assist co-ordination between the police and judiciary in all member states, to help combat crimes such as the trafficking of human beings.

▶ Introduced a regulation, since adopted by the International Maritime Organisation, prohibiting from 2005 the transporting of heavy petroleum products in single-hulled oil tankers.

▶ Committed €1 billion, via the European Water Fund, to improving water provision and management in developing countries.

▶ Funded over 300 projects, since 2000, to help combat domestic violence against women and children.

▶ Created six million new jobs in the EU since 1999.

EXPANDING THE EU

The process of new countries joining the European Community was named Enlargement. There have been five 'Enlargements' to date:

▶ In 1973 Denmark, Ireland and the UK joined (finally!)
▶ In 1981 Greece joined.
▶ In 1986 Spain and Portugal joined.
▶ In 1995 Austria, Sweden and Finland joined.
▶ In 2004 ten new countries joined: The Czech Republic, Slovakia, Poland, Slovenia, Malta, Hungary, Cyprus. Estonia, Latvia, and Lithuania.

So there are now 25 countries in the European Union. Countries that belong to the European Union are called member states.

THE 5TH ENLARGEMENT

The 5th Enlargement of 2004 was of an unprecedented scale. The size of the European Union community increased by 75 million people! It followed an earlier pledge (made in 1993) that any central or eastern European country would be welcome to join - 'as soon as the country is able to assume the obligations of membership by satisfying the economic and political conditions.' These conditions included improving democracy and human rights, and, of course, the opening up of economic markets.

BY THE WAY

The Government of Norway applied to join the European Economic Community in 1972 and 1992. Both times the Norwegians voted 'No' to membership in respective referendums.

The Swiss Government applied to join the European Economic Community in 1992, but withdrew its application after the Swiss public rejected membership of the European Economic Area. The Swiss Government tried again in 2001. The Swiss electorate voted a resounding 'NO!' - 76.7% of voters rejected the idea.

The Government of Iceland has never applied to join, which makes it unique.

THE UK's REFERENDUM

The 1975 the UK Government held a referendum, asking the British public whether it should remain in the European Economic Community.

It was a closely fought battle and pre-referendum polls predicted the anti-Europe campaigners would win. However, on the day, 67% voted in favour of remaining 'in Europe' against 33% who voted for withdrawal.

PREPARING FOR THE 5TH ENLARGEMENT

Formal preparations for the 5th Enlargement of 2004 began with the signing of The Treaty of Nice.

Applicants for the 5th Enlargement process were required to sign up to an Accession Partnership, which set out the short and medium term priorities they needed to fulfill to meet membership obligations. It also indicated the financial assistance the European Union would provide, and the conditions attached to this assistance.

Complex negotiations on many things, including voting rights for member states following the accession of the 5th Enlargement candidate countries, meant the Treaty of Nice was a VERY hard nut to crack.

Following its signing, member states had until December 2002 to ratify the treaty, in accordance with their own constitutional rules.

THE PROS AND CONS

Arguments that were given in favour of the 5th Enlargement:

▸ It will unite the continent and assist peace and stability.

▸ The Single Market will benefit from millions of new consumers.

▸ It will be easier to tackle common problems such as crime and illegal immigration.

▸ European Union membership will increase standards of living in new member countries.

▸ The process of Enlargement will make the European Union revise its policies and procedures, many of which badly needed updating.

Arguments that were given against:

▸ With 25 member states represented in the European Council, decision-making will be impossible.

▸ The European Commission alone will need 4000 new members of staff to cope with the extra bureaucracy.

▸ Cheap labour will flood into Western Europe unless immigration controls are put in place.

▸ Investment will flow eastwards whilst factories will close in the west.

▸ The economies of the east and west are just too diverse.

▸ European Union funds will be diverted from poorer western regions to new member states in central and eastern Europe.

THE IRISH REFERENDUM

The Irish Government had to rafity the Treaty of Nice via a referendum, which was held in June 2001. The Irish Government suffered a shock defeat! 54% voted No, and only 32% of the population bothered to vote at all. The European Union told Ireland the Treaty of Nice would not be re-opened for debate, and that a second Referendum must be held (and, er, won!)

(You see, Ireland's failure to ratify the Treaty would threaten a constitutional crisis in the European Union, and ultimately, delay the 5th Enlargement. - No pressure then!)

The main reason given for the Irish referendum result was a sense of general disillusionment about the European Union and the future direction it was taking.

SECOND TIME LUCKY

After the first referendum, The Irish Government told the European Union 'we genuinely need, at the national level, an extended period of reflection.'

A second referendum was held in October 2002, and the voters this time supported the Irish Government's ratification of The Treaty of Nice. (And many politicians across Europe were very, very relieved.)

MORE PROBLEMS

Just one week after the first Irish referendum on the Treaty of Nice, a further set back to the 5th Enlargement occurred. The European Council's Gothenburg Summit* attracted violent protests and street riots (15,000 protestors no less). The expansion and further political integration of Europe was becoming a bit of an issue for the people of Europe. Newspapers relished headlines such as 'EU LEADERS FEAR WRATH OF THE PEOPLE.' Afterwards European leaders admitted:

▸ There was growing public resistance across the European Union to further political integration.
▸ Disillusionment with the European Union was becoming a major problem in most member states.
▸ There was growing frustration at a perceived absence of clarity and openness in the way the European Union operates.

The overwhelming lesson appeared to be that national public opinion must NOT be taken for granted.

Nevertheless the European Council still declared at the end of the Gothenburg Summit that 'the Enlargement process is irreversible.' (Some said this was a bold and brave statement. Others said it was bloody stupid, given the circumstances.)

The European Council meets every six months for a 'Summit.' Their summits are always named after the town or city in which they are held.

MAY 1ST 2004

What were you doing on this day? On May 1st 2004 the 5th Enlargement finally happened, despite all the controversy surrounding it. Ten new countries and circa 75 million people joined the European Union.

Celebrations took place across the continent: not that I noticed many where I live. Which I think is a shame. Whatever we might think of the European Union, May 1st 2004 saw a continent formally divided by both the World War Two and the Cold War, politically united.

When you consider that eight of the new member states were ruled by communist dictators for decades, the 5th Enlargement does seem quite an historic achievement, don't you think?

AND THE POPULATION OF THE EXPANDED EUROPEAN UNION?

After May 1st 2004, it became approximately 456 million.

OFFICIAL LANGUAGES

The European Union now has 20 official languages - and lots of translators!

PS!

Bulgaria, Romania and Turkey applied to join the EU as part of the 5th Enlargement process. They might join later, once they are able to meet membership criteria.

SIZE AND POPULATION

The credentials of the member states are:

Member State	Population (millions)	Size (000s km2)
Germany	82.2	356.8
UK	59.8	242.5
France	59.5	550
Italy	57.8	301.2
Poland	38.6	313
Spain	39.5	504.7
The Netherlands	16.0	41.8
Portugal	10.0	92
Greece	10.6	131.9
Belgium	10.3	30.1
Czech Republic	10.3	79
Hungary	10.2	93
Sweden	8.9	450
Austria	8.1	88.9
Slovakia	5.4	49
Slovenia	5.4	49
Denmark	5.3	43
Finland	5.2	338
Ireland	3.8	70
Lithuania	3.5	65
Latvia	2.4	65
Estonia	1.4	45
Cyprus	0.8	9
Luxembourg	0.4	2.5
Malta	0.4	0.3

EUROPEAN UNION BUDGETS

A member state's size and population aren't direct determinants of how much it pays into the European Union's coffers. Budget contributions are weighted according to a member state's GNP, or Gross National Product (which is basically a country's national income).

The national incomes of member states are then compared to the European Union's combined income. As a (very general) rule of thumb, richer member states pay more and poorer member states pay less. An EU rule dictates that its overall budget must not exceed 1.27% of the combined GNPs of all member states.

HOW MUCH DOES THE EU SPEND?

In 2003 the EU had a budget of 99.7 billion euros. Although this sounds a lot of money to you and me, it equates to only 1.02% of the combined incomes of all member states. The European Union gets its income (called 'own resources') from:

▸ Taxes on agricultural products
▸ Customs duty (from the common customs tariff)
▸ VAT (a uniform rate is applied on the VAT base of each member state, currently this is 0.5%)
▸ Something called the 'fourth resource' - which is the individual contributions made by member states. (This provides approx. 50% of total EU income.)

MEMBER STATE CONTRIBUTIONS

2002 figures were the latest statistics available:

	% of Total Contributions	Contribution (€million)	Operational Balance*
Germany	22.6	17,582	-5,068
France	18.2	14,152	-2,184
Italy	14.5	11,279	-2,885
UK	13.1	10,153	-2,903**
Spain	8.4	6,551	+8,871
Netherlands	5.7	4,467	-2,188
Belgium	3.9	3,018	-256
Sweden	2.7	2,086	-747
Austria	2.3	1,809	-226
Denmark	2.2	1,688	-165
Greece	1.7	1,337	+3,388
Finland	1.5	1,185	-5.7
Portugal	1.5	1,187	+2,692
Ireland	1.3	1,018	+1,577
Luxembourg	0.2	184	-48.9

* 'Operational Balance' is the difference between what member states pay in contributions and what they receive back via different EU funding programmes. Some member states are 'net beneficiaries' (shown as a + figure) and others are 'net contributors' (shown as a - figure).

** This figure is after our UK rebate (see next page).

NB. The 5th Enlargement has meant considerable change will occur in the balance between what member states pay in and what they get out.

THE UK REBATE

Good news!

The UK is the only country to get a rebate from the European Union!

It is worth, typically, between £2 to £3 billion per annum, and is due to some nifty negotiating by Maggie Thatcher (bless her!).

The UK Rebate started in 1984 and is next up for 'discussion' in 2006. Word on the street is that the European Union simply won't be able to afford such a rebate any more. (And, in fairness I suppose, the other member states are a bit miffed by it.)

The UK has typically been a net contributor to the European Union - it puts in more money than it gets back.

The UK Rebate, simply described, means the UK can claim back two-thirds of the difference between what we contribute to the European Union and what we get back in subsidies and other European Union payments.

THE FINANCIAL PERSPECTIVE

The Financial Perspective is an agreement that sets out the maximum amount and the composition of foreseeable European Union expenditure. At the moment we are amidst a financial framework for the period 2000 - 2006. This was agreed in 1999. A main aim of the framework was to plan and provide for both the development of new EU policies and the 5th Enlargement, without having to change something called the 'own resources ceiling.' (This is the rule that states overall EU budgets mustn't exceed 1.27% of member state national incomes.) The Financial Perspective sets maximum spending ceilings for each budget area. A margin of error is left between these ceilings and the European Union's overall budget, to provide some financial flexibility. The seven budget headings are:

Budget Areas (with 2004 figures)	(€million)
Agriculture: the Common Agriculture Policy	42, 760
Structural Operations: funds to reduce inequalities across the regions of the EU.	29, 595
Internal Policies: addressing various projects and issues within the EU.	6,370
External Actions: for non-member countries worldwide, e.g. humanitarian aid.	4,590
Admin:	4,900
Reserves:	40
Aid to 5th Enlargement Countries	3,120

REFORM OF EU BUDGETS

The 5th Enlargement created the need to review the way European Union budgets are spent. There is widespread belief that the concept of the Single Market - particularly one with 25 member states - will only work if the European Union funding mechanisms are drastically reformed. The obvious target for reform was the Common Agricultural Policy (CAP), which was proposed by the French and established in 1962 to boost agricultural productivity. It is probably the European Union's most widely recognised activity .

And so it should be! Until recently, the CAP used circa 50% of the EU's entire annual budget! And, amazingly, 75% of this vast sum of money went to just 20% of Europe's farmers.

(And I don't mind telling you, of all the riveting research I carried out for this book, this figure was the one that made me swear out loud in my local Reference Library!)

THE UK's CAP PAYMENTS

In 2000, 21.7% of the CAP went to French farmers, 15.1% to German farmers, 12.4% to Italian farmers, and 8.4% to UK farmers. (It will therefore be no surprise to hear that France and Germany resisted any radical reform for as long as they could.)

REFORM OF THE COMMON AGRICULTURAL POLICY

In June 2003, European Union farm ministers adopted a fundamental reform of the CAP. It followed extensive negotiations, and will completely change the way the European Union supports the farming sector. Previously, subsidies were linked to productivity (hence farmers were encouraged to keep producing, despite the butter or wheat 'mountains' the policy generated).

As of 2005, farmers will instead get a 'single farm payment.' The payment will be linked to things such as respect for the environment, food safety, and animal and plant health/welfare.

Severing the link between production and subsidies is intended to make farmers more competitive and market-orientated.*

The reforms also proposed to cut the direct payments made to the EU's bigger farms, most of which are in the UK and Eastern Germany. (The National Farmers Union estimates that 580 farms in England will loose £62 million.)

The reforms also included changes to market policies and intervention prices for things such as butter, skimmed milk powder and cereals. If you'd like to know more, see the EU's server for more information (http://europa.eu.int).

As a New Zealander, can I just remind everyone that New Zealand farmers have survived without subsidies for over twenty years now. It can be done!

HOW EU VOTING WORKS

There are two key methods of decision making within the European Council.

With 'Unanimous Voting' any member state can impose their veto to block a decision or proposal. Because of this, 'stalemate' situations are common.

In the 'Qualified Majority Voting system' a member state's population affects the number of votes they are allocated in the European Council. One or more member state can disagree with a proposal, but be overruled by a majority. Qualified Majority Voting was introduced as a means of overcoming the 'stalemate' problem associated with the Unanimous Voting process. However, Unanimous Voting is still used for the most significant decisions.

NB. A *gargantuan* fight occurred in relation to the allocation of Qualified Majority Voting votes following the 5th Enlargement!

NB. Later on we're going to talk about the new Constitution for Europe. It is proposing a new method of decision making altogether, called Double Majority. It means member states will have less opportunity to use their national veto to block decisions.

QUALIFIED MAJORITY VOTING

Following the 5th Enlargement, the votes attributed to member states for the purposes of Qualified Majority Voting are as listed below. There are 321 votes in all. A European Council decision is adopted if at least 232 votes are received.

Member State	Votes
Germany	29
UK	29
France	29
Italy	29
Spain	27
Poland	27
The Netherlands	13
Greece	12
Czech Republic	12
Belgium	12
Hungary	12
Portugal	12
Sweden	10
Austria	10
Slovakia	7
Denmark	7
Finland	7
Ireland	7
Lithuania	7
Latvia	4
Slovenia	4
Estonia	4
Cyprus	4
Luxembourg	4
Malta	3

ECONOMIC & MONETARY UNION

An Economic and Monetary Union (EMU) was included in the Maastricht Treaty as a founding principle of the new European Union. EMU was a more complex form of economic integration than the European Economic Community had ever attempted, involving the adoption of a **single currency**. Three steps were agreed for the establishment of a single currency:

Step One: was the on-going development of the Single Market, which would lay the solid foundations necessary for an Economic and Monetary Union.

Step Two: started in January 1994. Member states were asked to start making their economies 'suitable' for the Economic and Monetary Union. A number of 'Convergence Criteria' were agreed, which would ensure that participating member states would share a common basis of financial stability. Simply speaking, these criteria required a member state to have low inflation, sound public finances, and a stable exchange rate.

Step Three: started on January 1st 1999, when the single currency was introduced in those member states who met the necessary Convergence Criteria. Euro notes and coins weren't introduced for public circulation at this time. Instead, the exchange rates between existing member state currencies and the euro were locked. The European Central Bank became responsible for interest rates in participating member states.

Euro notes and coins were introduced on January 1st 2002.

THE OPT OUT

During The Maastricht Treaty negotiations, the UK and Denmark secured the right to opt out of the single currency, even if and when their economies met the Convergence Criteria. This is important, because it means either country may choose to never adopt the euro, and won't be in breach of their Maastricht Treaty ratification by doing so.

The UK didn't meet the Convergence Criteria necessary to join the single currency in January 1999. Although the UK's inflation level and government deficit were on target, the erratic exchange rate of sterling was a bit of a problem.

REMEMBER CHANCELLOR LAMONT?

The European Exchange Rate Mechanism (ERM) was established in 1979 to make exchange rates between countries in the European Economic Community more stable. The UK spectacularly withdrew from the ERM in 1992, and didn't rejoin it. (It was all a bit of a drama at the time.)

After leaving the ERM, sterling experienced significant fluctuations in value. And, as joining the single currency would mean fixing the pound's exchange rate against other European currencies for all time, the government decided it wasn't an idea worth pursuing.

'ERM2'

The Exchange Rate Mechanism was refined in 1997, in acknowledgement of its shortcomings that assisted the 1992 crisis.

The refined ERM is now called ERM2.

Member states that elect not to join the single currency have the voluntary option to join ERM2 instead. By doing so, their national currencies are pegged to the euro (which will assist in creating the exchange rate stability they need as a condition to joining the single currency).

The UK Government has to date made no public commitment to rejoin ERM2.

WHO ADOPTED THE EURO?

The following member states joined the single currency in January 1999:

Austria, Belgium, Finland, France, Germany, Ireland, Italy Luxembourg, the Netherlands, Portugal, and Spain.

In January 2001 Greece also joined the single currency. In September 2000 the people of Denmark voted no to the euro in a referendum. In June 2003 the people of Sweden voted no to the euro in a referendum.

THE 'EUROZONE'

The eurozone is the term given to all member states who have signed up to, and are using, the single currency. To keep us on our toes, it seems some people use the phrase 'euro area' or 'euroland' instead.

EURO CONVERSION RATES

These are the official euro conversion rates agreed on December 31st 1998 for the first wave of participants. (I've rounded the five decimal places up ...)

1 euro =

1936.3	Italian Lira
200.5	Portuguese Escudo
166.4	Spanish Peseta
40.3	Belgian Franc
40.3	Luxembourg Franc
13.7	Austrian Schilling
6.5	French Franc
5.9	Finish Markka
2.2	Netherlands Guilder
1.9	German Deutschmark
0.78	Irish Punt

The Greek Drachma entered at 340.75. Meanwhile, to date the pound has fluctuated between a low of 0.57p (May 2000) and a high of 72p (May 2003).

THE END OF SOMETHING OLD

The French franc and the Dutch guilder were both over 600 years old. The Greek drachma had existed in one form or another - excepting the odd period of foreign occupation - for over 2500 years! The Athenian drachma - an earlier version known as 'silver owls' - reigned supreme in the ancient world for almost 600 years.

Indeed, when Athens defeated Aegina in 456BC they imposed the circulation of silver owls and demanded the territory stop minting their own currency, known as 'turtles.' How ironic that, a few millenniums later, the drachma disappeared overnight after the wielding of pens rather than swords!

EURO CHEEK!

Some manufacturers saw the introduction of the euro as a good excuse to Take the Michael! After the launch, Germany's leading consumer group found that 100 common consumer items had risen in price (some by up to 50%). In Ireland the Consumer Association of Ireland published a list of 'euro rip-offs' (some Dublin pubs increased the price of a pint by 12%, SHAME on them!). In Belgium prices increased by an average of 7% across 1500 everyday products. Governments are also guilty. Car parking charges in Paris went up by a third. And in Brussels parking metre charges went up by 17%.

SINGLE CURRENCY, SINGLE INTEREST RATE

This is an important point to note about the single currency: member states in the eurozone have their interest rate set by the European Central Bank (ECB). - So there is one interest rate applied throughout all eurozone countries.

The second important point is this: the European Central Bank is an independent central bank, so bankers – not politicians - make decisions on interest rates.

The European Central Bank was established under terms agreed in The Maastricht Treaty. It is responsible for the monetary policy of the single currency, including managing foreign exchange operations and currency reserves.

Member state governments appoint the ECB President for an eight-year term. Once appointed, he or she is politically unaccountable. The ECB Council has 18 members, including the governors of member state central banks. It operates a 'one member one vote' method of decision making. The first ECB President was Wim Duisenberg. The current President is Jean-Claude Trichet.

The European Central Bank is based in Frankfurt.

INTEREST RATES

The significance of member states handing over the control of their interest rates to the European Central Bank is:

National governments will loose an important 'tool' in the management of their domestic economies, because, they will loose the ability to raise or lower interest rates to respond to domestic economic conditions.

This is one of the key issues on which the 'euro debate' in the UK is being fought.

THE BANK OF ENGLAND

Here's an interesting thing! In June 1998 - about the same time the European Central Bank was getting sorted - the UK Government handed the control of the UK's interest rate to the Bank of England.

The Bank of England Act 1998 gave the Bank 'operational responsibility' for setting interest rates. Decisions are taken by a Monetary Policy Committee, which comprises the Bank's Governor and two Deputy Governors, two Bank Executive Directors, and four 'experts' (who are appointed by the Chancellor).

MANAGEMENT TARGETS

The European Central Bank's sole mandate is to pursue price stability through controlling inflation.

It has no formal or legal obligation to consider the impact of its policies on employment and economic growth – unlike the US Federal Reserve. Some economists (and politicians) have voiced concern that this is an out-dated and dangerous approach to monetary policy management. The European Central Bank Council have constantly defended their focus on price stability. They argue that the best contribution monetary policy can make to growth and employment lies in promoting stable prices. It's then up to individual governments to utilise this stable price climate to maximise growth and employment in their own countries.

INFLATION

The European Central Bank works towards an objective of 2% inflation. Since its creation it has been involved in one, long, inflation melodrama …

In March and April 2001 the ECB faced intense pressure to lower its interest rate, in the wake of the economic downturn in the US and Japan. The ECB chose not to do so, and was severely criticised by many significant and important folk.

DEFENDING ITS POLICIES

The ECB defended itself at the time by saying:

▶   A rate cut wasn't justified in the face of the eurozone's above-target inflation rate.

▶   We don't do knee-jerk reactions to political pressure.

▶   Lowering interest rates to give a 'short-term monetary stimulus' would not assist its 'long-term stable growth trajectory,' and would ultimately undermine the ECB's credibility.

More pointedly, Wim Duisenberg said, 'The only way to stimulate the economic growth potential of the euro-zone economy is through the application everywhere in Europe of structural reforms [to markets] – *not through monetary policy.'*

THE POLITICIANS SPEAK UP

In June 2001, members of the European Parliament's Economic & Monetary Affairs Committee recommended the ECB rethink its inflation target, citing their concern that high interest was restricting eurozone growth.

But the ECB was under no obligation to respond.

INTEREST RATE CHANGES

In May 2001 the ECB finally responded to its critics' pleas and cut interest rates in the eurozone by a quarter point. Further rate cuts followed (which seemed to be less symbolic). Then, an interesting moment occurred in June 2003. The ECB dropped interest rates to 2% on the same day that the Bank of England decided to keep UK interest rates at 3.75%.

The rate cut in the eurozone was needed as 'an aggressive attempt to kick-start the eurozone's floundering economy.' (Germany's especially - though the point was made that other countries, such as Ireland, didn't need an interest rate cut at all, thanks very much). Meanwhile, the UK economy didn't need a rate cut either. Some newspapers were quick to point out how lucky we were to still have control over ours.

TO SUMMARISE . . .

▶ The ECB's role is to provide a stable foundation for growth, but the burden of getting on and creating economic growth falls on others (politicians, business leaders and so on.)

▶ The ECB creates the long-term stability that provides a 'favourable climate' for investment and structural reform decisions – decisions that politicians have to make.

▶ The ECB is not directly responsible for economic growth or employment; its key objective is long-term stability.

SOME COMMON OPINION

I've read lots of analytical articles about the ECB (and yes, they were a bit dull.) The main concerns people seem to have are:

▸ The ECB is unaccountable.

▸ The ECB's remit of low inflation is pursued at the risk of a decline in growth and rise in unemployment.

▸ The ECB uses a weighted average of inflation in all 12 eurozone countries, which doesn't accurately depict the regional differences in their economies. This, together with the ECB Council's one member–one vote system means reaching a consensus is difficult, as Council members vote with their own national interests in mind.

▸ Inflation is measured using historical data, whereas the management of growth and employment requires the assessment of future trends.

▸ The ECB's inflation ceiling of 2% is an unrealistic target. (Though some do believe this is a bold and brave target and it should be commended.) A 2% target is lower, for example, than Germany's average inflation for any extended period during the entire 20th century.

▸ The ECB's 2% target isn't flexible, yet the eurozone contains 12 broad and differing economies. (The Chancellor, Gordon Brown, hinted once that the ECB should study the Bank of England's approach to inflation - it sets a minimum and maximum ceiling.)

UK VERSUS THE EUROZONE

You may well ask what the big deal is about losing control of interest rates, when the UK Government has handed control over to the Bank of England anyway? In fact, the UK Government has retained an indirect influence on interest rates by setting the Bank of England an inflation target in each Budget. They have also maintained an opt-out of the agreement in 'extreme economic conditions,' or if war breaks out, for example.

Also, the Bank of England need only consider its domestic economy (and how global trends may affect it). In comparison, the European Central Bank must consider what is best for the collective economy of the entire eurozone when setting interest rates.

INFLATION!

Incase you haven't yet figured this one out yet … member states signed up to the euro share one interest rate, but **the rate of inflation within each member state will be different.**

The Economic and Monetary Union aims to reduce variations in inflation between member states. Participating governments are expected to manage their domestic economies appropriately so as to keep inflation low.

SOME EXAMPLES OF INFLATION

In February 2004 annual inflation figures for the EU were:

Sweden	0.2%
Finland	0.4%
Denmark	0.7%
Germany	0.8%
Belgium	1.2%
The Netherlands	1.3%
United Kingdom	1.3%
Austria	1.5%
EU 15 average	1.5%
France	1.9%
Portugal	2.1%
Spain	2.2%
Ireland	2.2%
Italy	2.4%
Luxembourg	2.4%
Greece	2.6%

NB. Figures are pre 5th Enlargement so do not include the ten new member states.

[Source: Eurostat - the European Union statisticians]

THE STABILITY & GROWTH PACT

Governments of member states participating in the single currency are set borrowing limits – to prevent one country behaving in a reckless manner which threatens the wider eurozone economy. The rules on government borrowing were set out initially in The Maastricht Treaty, and were refined in 1997.

So if you hear someone blather on about the 'Stability & Growth Pact' this is what they're talking about - the eurozone's rules on government borrowing.

THE DETERRENT

The Stability & Growth Pact established sanctions and fines for any member state that:

▶ works up an annual budget deficit in excess of 3% of its Gross Domestic Product (GDP).

▶ has national debt in excess of 60% of its GDP.

▶ has inflation rates outside of agreed parameters.

Any member state in breach of the Stability & Growth Pact must hand over 0.2% of its GDP to the European Union, which is held as a non-interest bearing deposit. If the conditions of the Stability & Growth Pact aren't met within two years, the deposit becomes a fine, and isn't returned.

IS IT SENSIBLE?

Some economists believe the Stability & Growth Pact encourages counterproductive economic management. What this means - apparently - is this ... If an economy is suffering a downturn, governments often borrow money to boost the economy and balance their books. However, eurozone governments will be forced to raise taxes and reduce expenditure instead (so they can balance the Government's books), both of which will worsen their economic downturn.

THEORY V. REALITY

The Stability & Growth Pact also tells off member states if they create too much of a national budget surplus. In February 2001, Ireland made history by being the first eurozone member state to be told to amend its budget plans by the EU. Ireland's budget – a surplus one - was criticised as being 'expansionary and pro-cyclical and therefore inconsistent with the EU's 2000 broad guidelines.' (Eh?)

In simple terms, the EU put pressure on Ireland to reduce public spending or increase taxes, so as to lower inflation and slow economic growth. The Irish Government said to the European Union, 'Feck off ya big eejits.'

(Just kidding, of course they didn't. They said, 'Our Budget is prudent and fiscally sound, so please go away' ... or something like that.)

OK, IT AIN'T WORKING . . .

The media's analysis of Ireland's reprimand was considerable. Ireland's budget surplus was approx. 4% of GDP. However, according to The Stability & Growth Pact, member states should have been running a surplus budget - because Europe was in a phase of economic growth.

And what about the other member states who hadn't managed a budget surplus at all, when they should have? (France, Germany and Italy were all running budget deficits at the time of Ireland's reprimand.)

Following the Ireland fiasco, Germany and France eventually got 'told off' as well, for running deficit budgets. Then, after they risked being fined for the *third successive year*, France and Germany forced the suspension of the Stability & Growth Pact's sanctions mechanism. (Er, isn't this cheating?)

Since then, the fiscal rules governing the eurozone have been 'in limbo.' Meanwhile, at the time of writing - April 2004 - the European Commission is taking the European Council to court (the European Court of Justice no less), to challenge the European Council's decision to suspend penalties. If the Commission wins it could mean punitive financial penalties for France and Germany.

Formal discussions on reforming the Stability & Growth Pact are scheduled to take place in 2005.

THE TRICKY BIT

So, here's a question for you: how will governments manage domestic economies within the eurozone?

As you now know, the rules of the Economic and Monetary Union mean national governments are unable to lower or raise interest rates independently of other eurozone member states, even though their own domestic conditions might require it. To understand the consequences of this we need to learn some basic economic principles. (Don't worry, I'll be real quick ...)

HOW TO MANAGE ECONOMIES . . .

There are many inter-related things that determine how economies perform. What follows is a very basic explanation, using the basic ingredients of an economy, which are:

▸ Interest rates
▸ Inflation
▸ Currency exchange rates
▸ Taxation and public spending (called fiscal policy)
▸ Unemployment.

P.S. *Remember too that global economic trends influence domestic trends.*
DISCLAIMER: *There are numerous other, highly complex inter-relations that influence the management and performance of an economy. If you want the complex details you won't find them in this book – go do an MBA.*

GROSS DOMESTIC PRODUCT

Gross Domestic Product - or GDP - is the most commonly used 'yardstick' of a country's economic performance. It measures the *volume* of goods and service produced over a period of time (e.g., annually).

Nominal GDP is the value of the goods and services produced in the specified period, at *current prices.*

The *value* of the volume of goods and services produced is then adjusted to a base year price, so annual comparisons can be made. This is called Real GDP.

Why am I bothering you with this? Because the difference between Real GDP and Nominal GDP is i*nflation* (that is, how much prices have increased).

WE ALL PLAY A ROLE

Part of the 'how to measure GDP' formula is the measurement of *annual consumer expenditure.* Therefore we influence GDP when we decide how much of our disposable income to *spend* rather than save. And, typically, we make the decision to save or spend based on the *interest rates* offered for our savings, and how these rates compare to *inflation.*

WHY IS HIGH INFLATION SO BAD?

Economies can be in a period of growth, or a period of decline (referred to as cycles). The knack in balancing an economy is to maintain growth, low unemployment and high spending, *without creating high inflation.*

High inflation means prices are rising. Which means we get less for our money (called the *erosion of purchasing power*). And that's bad! High inflation also causes uncertainty. And markets hate uncertainty. Investment tends to suffer, and generally, the national economy becomes less competitive on the world market.

INCASE YOU CAN'T REMEMBER?

In 1980 inflation in the UK was 20%! In 1990 it was 9%. These days it's only 2% or thereabouts. We're currently living through the longest sustained period of low inflation for decades. So the European Union has every reason to wish for the Economic & Monetary Union to sustain low inflation across Europe.

(In other words, it's not some whimsical goal thought up by some bored European Union bureaucrat, if that's what you were thinking?)

THE INFLATIONARY CYCLE

High inflation is caused by rising prices. Prices rise, generally, because *demand* for goods and services exceeds available supply. Or, prices may rise because of a sudden, sharp increase in the price of a raw material (such as oil).

Now, watch this (simplified) chain of events:

Companies increase productivity to try and meet demand.

Labour costs rise (increased overtime or shortage of workers can cause wages to go up).

If labour costs rise, or the price of a raw ingredient rises, companies increase the price of goods to keep their desired profit margins.

Or, firms might exploit a period of high demand for goods and increase their profit mark up.

Prices rise.

Workers demand an increase in wages (to keep up with rising prices).

And thus the vicious cycle spirals upwards!

THE ROLE OF UNEMPLOYMENT

The extent to which inflation follows this 'upward inflationary spiral' depends on the rate of unemployment at the time the spiral is set in motion. Most economists believe an economy has what's called a *natural rate of unemployment* at times of stable inflation and stable wages. In other words, there's always going to be a certain amount of people without work, for whatever reason. If unemployment is above the natural rate, there will be lots of unemployed people wanting jobs, so there will be less pressure on companies to increase wages. Hence the inflationary spiral should be easier to control.

UNEMPLOYMENT IN EUROPE

The problem is, unemployment rates vary in member states across Europe. Therefore, member states will have to manage rising inflation on uneven playing fields, so to speak.

The Single Market aims to ease the movement of workers across Europe, because a flexible labour force (how quickly and easily workers can find work and companies can fill vacancies) is a good tool in the management of economies. Theoretically, a flexible labour force would assist in balancing natural rates of unemployment and cushioning 'economic shocks' in individual member states.

(Are you keeping up?!)

THE IMPORTANCE OF LABOUR REFORM

Critics of the single currency stress that it won't succeed unless European citizens are willing to travel abroad to find work – and at the moment most of us aren't. Only 0.4% of European Union citizens move to another member state to work every year (in the USA inter-state labour movement is six times higher).

Considerable barriers remain to labour movement in the European Union. For example:

▶ tax issues (tax rates aren't harmonised across the EU)
▶ pensions (they're not portable)
▶ lack of mutual recognition of some qualifications
▶ language and cultural differences
▶ the different levels of 'power' held by Trade Unions in various member states
▶ some immigration restrictions (e.g. people from the countries who recently joined the European Union in the 5th Enlargement face a number of restrictions to working in member states in western Europe.)

Therefore, in the European Union only the highly skilled or highly motivated tend to move. Because of this, the reform of European Union labour markets is a key objective that member states are currently trying to progress.

ECONOMIC 'TOOLS'

By joining the single currency, eurozone governments have lost two of the 'tools' they could traditionally use (through adjusting them) to manage their economies:

▶   interest rates
▶   foreign currency exchange rates (devaluing a currency is a means of boosting an economy).

So what happens when a particular member state's domestic economy goes into a boom or recession that isn't shared by other member state economies? (Because, if the boom or recession, or threat thereof, isn't shared by other member states, the European Central Bank may not adjust eurozone interest rates to help.) How capable will governments be at adjusting the remaining items in their 'economic tool kit' (e.g. public spending and taxation), in order to rebalance the economy?

TAXATION

Taxation is, of course, a vital ingredient of a government's fiscal policy. At the moment member states are free to make their own taxation policies.

The European Union has set itself the goal of harmonising taxation across all member states – particularly VAT, excise and income taxes – but there are ENORMOUS political and practical barriers to this ever happening.

TAXATION IN THE EU

The uphill battle facing harmonisation of EU taxes is due to the vast differences in taxation policies across Europe. Some member states have a high tax – high spend policy (e.g. France, where the public trains actually work thanks to massive state subsidies). And some member states tax specific things more than others (e.g. in the UK we pay considerably higher levies on fuels). Or, in Germany, for example, the Government taxes pension contributions, but not the resulting pension (whereas in the UK we do the opposite).

Company tax in some of the 5th Enlargement member states is less than half that of company tax levies in the UK or Germany. (In Estonia company tax has been reduced to 0% to encourage new business investment!)

Some folk argue that tax harmonisation is critical to the success of the Economic and Monetary Union. Others argue that it isn't; that taxation should remain in the control of national governments.

Others argue that it's academic anyway, because it will take decades of controversy to harmonise taxation policies throughout the European Union, and the politicians won't have sufficient will to see it through.

'PRICE PARITY'

There is a little economic ditty called *Purchasing Power Parity*. It assumes that market forces will encourage a unit of currency to have the same purchasing power in all countries. Supporters of the single currency argue it will expose price transparency and deliver more competitive prices to all consumers. Others argue that products don't respond to the 'Purchasing Power Parity' theory because of differences in VAT, labour costs, and productivity rates.

In April 2000 *The Economist* magazine compared the prices of Big Mac hamburgers, as a means of assessing 'purchasing power parity.' A Big Mac in the UK was 19.7% overvalued against the $US base price. In comparison a French Big Mac was only 3.8% overvalued, and in Germany a Big Mac was 6.1% undervalued. Sadly, I couldn't locate an updated Mac-ometer.

However, in May 2002 the European Union's Internal Markets Commissioner published a scoreboard showing, amongst other things, that Italians pay twice as much for Heinz Tomato Ketchup as Germans do, while in the UK we pay 70% more for Colgate toothpaste than the Spanish. Outrageous!

Meanwhile, in 2003 the same Ikea mirror cost the equivalent of US$32 in Spain, $22 in Belgium, $21 in France, $13 in Denmark, and $25 in the UK.

'THE LISBON AGENDA'

The Lisbon Summit of 2000 set out a ten-year framework of economic reform for the European Union. Its declared objective was to turn Europe into the world's most competitive and dynamic, knowledge-based economy by 2010, with targets of 3% growth and 20 million new jobs.

The agreed 'Things To Do' list was ambitious by anyone's standards. For example:

▶ postal services and energy markets to be liberalised (to do away with Government monopolies in some member states)
▶ an EU wide patent to be established
▶ a single market for financial services (which includes over 40 pieces of legislation!)
▶ a single European Sky (a uniform system of air traffic control)
▶ reform of welfare systems
▶ several new Employment Directives.

All of these things involve member state governments passing some of their decision-making powers to the European Union.

'THE OPEN METHOD OF CO-ORDINATION'

Yes, I know. What a phrase! This one refers to the new form of decision-making brewed up at the Lisbon Summit. It's an alternative to the complex decision-making normally adopted by the European Council, and the complex process of making and enforcing European Union laws.

Because economic reform is such an important objective, the 'Open Method of Co-ordination' allows member states to adopt goals and indicators as a means of measuring their progress. The benchmarking of member states monitors who is and isn't doing what The Lisbon Agenda requires.

The theory was that 'peer group pressure' will bring 'naughty' member states into line if their goals and indicators don't meet expectations and benchmarking standards. An annual 'Scorecard' of progress in each member state is reviewed each Spring.

To date, however, it has been evident that national priorities and concerns are hindering implementation of the Lisbon Agenda. (Spain and the UK are arguing over airspace over Gilbraltor, France is delaying the deregulation of its precious energy markets, and a complete deadlock still exists over an European Union patent, for example.)

THE LATEST SCORECARD

In March 2004, the fourth 'Scorecard' of the Lisbon Agenda was produced. As the ten-year programme's half way mark of 2005 was fast approaching, there was considerable interest in the results. The 'Lisbon Scorecard IV' rated the performance of member state reforms. Each of five broad areas included specific issues, and for each issue 'Heroes' and 'Villains' were identified. The issues, and the score awarded for overall efforts across the European Union, were:

Innovation:
▸ Information Society, B-
▸ Research & Development, C

Liberalisation:
▸ Telecoms and Utilities, C+ (UK = Hero!)
▸ Transport, C+
▸ Financial and other services, C+ (UK = Hero!)

Enterprise:
▸ Business start-up environment, C
▸ Regulatory burden, C
▸ State Aid competition policy, C+

Employment and Social Inclusion:
▸ Bringing people into the workforce, C-
▸ Upgrading skills, C
▸ Modernising social protection*, B- (UK = Villain, for social exclusion)

Sustainable Environment:
▸ Climate change, C-
▸ Natural environment, C+

(Worst in class was Italy, Villain in 6 areas.)
(Best in class was Sweden, Hero in 8.)
* this includes the tricky task of overhauling pensions systems.

ECONOMIC REFORM SO FAR: SOME BAD NEWS

▶ GDP in the European Union grew by just 0.8% in 2003, and it has been acknowledged that the economic gap between Europe and the US won't be closed by 2010.

▶ Employment growth in the European Union ground to a halt in 2003. The European Union will 'almost certainly' fail to reach its goal of 70% employment by 2010.

▶ The European Union still invests considerably less on research and development than the US and Japan.

▶ Progress in the opening up of energy markets has been 'painfully slow.'

SOME GOOD NEWS

▶ France and Germany both pushed through painful pension and labour market reforms during 2003.

▶ The economic strength of Denmark, Finland and Sweden.

▶ Internet access in the former EU15 member states more than doubled between 2000 and 2003, to 47% (compared to 54% in the US*)

▶ Good progress was made in increasing competition in the telecoms market.

(* And here's a good piece of dinner party trivia for you: which country do you think has the highest rate of internet access in the world? Iceland! - 69%.)

POOR GRADES: SHALL WE GIVE UP?

The 'Lisbon Scorecard IV' was discussed at the March 2004 Brussels Summit. No one was very impressed with the grades. European leaders admitted that their grand plan to unseat the US as the world's leading economic power by 2010 had lost its credibility.

What people said …

Jacques Chirac, French President:
'Despite the charms of the city of Lisbon, I don't think this idea seems to have caught on.'

Romano Prodi, European Commission President:
'There is no point setting these objectives if there is no will to meet them. I can't really expect any major progress.'

The Confederation of British Industry:
Foot-dragging by member states was 'making a mockery' of the Lisbon Agenda.

So we will have to wait and see what happens with this one …

(Watch out for future Scorecards every March!)

THE FIVE POINT TEST

Whilst declining to join the single currency in January 1999, the UK's Labour Government of the day highlighted five key economic tests, upon which a future decision to join the single currency would be based:

1. Despite any long-term benefits to joining the single currency, are business cycles and economic structures compatible? Can UK citizens and other Europeans live comfortably with euro interest rates on a permanent basis? (Called The Convergence Test.)

2. If problems do emerge, is there sufficient flexibility to deal with them? This test refers to issues like prices, wages, labour markets and unemployment. (The Flexibility Test.)

3. Will joining the Economic & Monetary Union create better conditions for firms making long-term decisions to invest in the UK? (The Investment Test.)

4. How will adopting the single currency affect the UK's financial services? (The City Test.)

5. Will joining the Economic & Monetary Union help to promote higher growth, stability and a lasting increase in jobs? (The Jobs & Growth Test.)

ECONOMIC TESTS OR USEFUL POLITICAL AID?

From the moment it was set out, the Chancellor's Five Point Test was criticised. It's too vague and allows Yes or No answers that can't be quantified, people said. Some suggested the Five Point Test was merely a bunch of reasons thrown together to justify the Government's decision not to join the single currency in January 1999. Some suggested it would handily allow the UK Government to call a referendum whenever it wants. Others said it made the decision to join the euro an *economic decision*, when in fact the single currency is a *political project*. Others said the Five Point Test was sound and comprehensive, and was as good a starting point as any for such a huge piece of decision-making.

THE 2001 ELECTIONS

Many people argued that the whole 'euro debate' was too focused on the economy, and not focused enough on issues of sovereignty, nationality, our constitution, our civil rights as British citizens, etc. In response to this criticism, the Labour Government campaigned for the 2001 General Election saying that, once the five-point-test was passed, there would be a **national referendum** on whether or not the UK should join the euro. A national referendum would provide a forum in which all related issues could be debated.

WHAT THE OTHER PARTIES SAID

The Conservative Party said they would keep the pound for the next five-year term of Parliament, after which the benefits of joining the single currency would be re-assessed. Because they would not be proposing to join the single currency, a referendum on the issue would not be held. The Liberal Democrats committed to holding a referendum on the euro.

LANDSLIDE!

The Tories made Europe a key platform of their 2001 election campaign. The Labour Party, in contrast, tried to mention the euro as little as possible. The polls regularly showed the majority of voters being against the euro, but also regularly showed the euro as a minor consideration in the election race. (In one poll, the euro was ranked last in a list of eleven key issues!) Voters constantly prioritised domestic issues - public services, health, and education for example.

Following Labour's election victory, a new Conservative Party leadership battle commenced. Michael Portillo refused to water down his anti-euro stance, and was prematurely removed from the leadership race. The final battle was fought between Kenneth Clarke (pro-euro) and Ian Duncan-Smith (anti-euro). So for one reason and another, the British public had euro-politics in their newspapers for the entire summer of 2001. (Which most of us found very tedious.)

REFERENDUM: YES OR NO?

Following the Labour victory, attention quickly turned to Labour's promised referendum on the single currency. When would they call it?

The markets read Mr Blair's significant election majority as a clue that the voters weren't too bothered about saving the pound. In the week after the election, the pound fell to a fifteen year low against the dollar, as the markets assumed a referendum was near. (Business and economists said at the time that the pound would need to fall by up to 15% before membership of the single currency would became viable).

Following the election, Sir Eddie George, Governor of The Bank of England, reminded us that driving down the pound would 'stoke inflationary pressures.'

The Government stressed that their priority for the new Parliament was to deliver promised improvements to public services.

The euro thing will have to wait, they said.

(How right they were!)

EURO SECURITY

In the approach to the launch of the euro on the continent, national mints across Europe frantically printed 14.5 billion new euro banknotes, and 50 billion new coins! Such was the scale of the operation, the army assisted in several countries as the loot was stored in secret locations. The police and army operation that guarded the distribution of the money was of an unprecedented peace-time scale.

The first euro theft was as long ago as 1998, when hologram printing plates were stolen off a plane during a flight between Germany and France.

There were several armed robberies across the continent during 'E-Day' deliveries, but not nearly as many as police had feared. The most spectacular robbery occurred prior to E-Day, when €1.2m was stolen in Germany (though most of the money was subsequently recovered.)

PUBLICITY IS KEY!

In September 2001, the European Central Bank launched a publicity, advertising and training campaign (price tag = €80 million!), to help prepare participating member states for their new notes and coins.

The slogan: "The euro. Our money."

THE FIVE-POINT TEST REPORT

So … onwards to June 2003, when Gordon Brown delivered an eagerly awaited 'verdict' on his Five-Point Test. Was the nation ready to join the single currency?

The Chancellor delivered the following to the nation:
- A 246 page Assessment
- A 171 page Changeover Plan
- 18 supplementary studies, comprising over 2000 pages and 1.5 million words.

Fear not! For you, I have prepared a summary version:
- The Convergence Test   Fail
- The Flexibility Test   Fail
- The Investment Test   Fail
- The City Test   Pass! (Hoorah!)
- The Jobs & Growth Test   Fail.

Meeting the requirements of the Convergence and Flexibility tests was critical. Because these tests failed, we automatically failed the Investment and Jobs & Growth tests.

However, the Chancellor's verdict was presented as an 'It's Not A No, It's A Not Yet' decision. The Five Tests would be reassessed, he said. Meanwhile, the Government would start on the economic reforms necessary to make conditions satisfactory for our adopting the euro.

WORK STILL TO BE DONE

The Chancellor said that the UK needed to:

▶ bring our inflation target into line with the eurozone's (we have since adopted the type of 'inflation index' used in the eurozone.)

▶ reform our mortgage system (encourage more long-term, fixed-rate mortgages, so we are less vulnerable to interest rate changes.)

▶ reform our planning and house building systems (we need more houses!)

▶ consult on new tax policies (which will be required once control of our interest rate is given to the European Central Bank.)

▶ have the EU reform its Stability & Growth Pact.

▶ encourage regional pay-setting for the public sector (hugely controversial ... don't get the Unions started on this one).

STERLING EXCHANGE RATES

One of The Treasury's supporting studies mentioned that an exchange rate of 73p to the euro might be a good exchange rate for entry to the single currency. Opinion varied on this figure. Some experts felt 73p to the euro was an entirely realistic target, whilst others did not.

(And if experts can never agree on anything, what chance do we stand?)

INFORMATION OVERLOAD!

The Press dedicated pages and pages to The Chancellor's verdict on the euro. What did it really mean? Would we ever join? I shan't make you endure a summary of the extensive amount of postulating that took place. However, if you're interested, go to your library and seek out copies of national newspapers dated June 10th 2003. Or, you could visit the Treasury's website: www.hm-treasury.gov.uk. For now, the supporting studies are available on-line. Choose from:

▸ The Five Tests framework
▸ Analysis of European & UK business cycles and shocks
▸ Estimates of equilibrium exchange rates for sterling against the euro
▸ Housing, consumption and Economic and Monetary Union (EMU)
▸ EMU and the monetary transmission mechanism
▸ Modelling the transition to EMU
▸ Modelling shocks and adjustment mechanisms in EMU
▸ EMU and labour market flexibility
▸ The exchange rate and macroeconomic adjustment
▸ EMU and the cost of capital
▸ EMU and business sectors
▸ The location of financial activity and the euro
▸ EMU and trade
▸ Prices and EMU
▸ The United States as a monetary union
▸ Policy frameworks in the UK and EMU
▸ Submissions on EMU from leading academics
▸ Fiscal stabilisation and EMU - a discussion paper.

HOUSING

Housing was highlighted as a particular area of concern following the Chancellor's Five Point Test verdict. The concerns were:

▸ The UK has a considerably higher proportion of home owners with variable-rate mortgages (almost 40% in 2003, down from 70% in 2002), which means our economy is more sensitive to interest rate changes. In Germany, by comparison, over 80% of homeowners have fixed-rate mortgages of over 5 years' duration. In France over 90% of homeowners have at least 5 year fixed-rate mortgages.

▸ We have a high level of owner occupation compared to other member states (69% of housing stock). In Germany, for example, home ownership accounts for only 40% of the housing stock.

▸ The UK has seen a long-term increase in 'real' house prices. Among larger EU countries, only Spain has seen increases comparable to the UK.

▸ Mortgage debt in the UK is well above the EU average (equivalent to 60% of the UK's gross domestic product - the EU average is 40%). Only Denmark and the Netherlands have a higher level.

▸ New housebuilding is currently about 170,000 new homes per year. It is at its lowest peacetime level since the 1920s.

The Government is looking at a number of measures to help stabilise the UK housing market. These include promoting longer term fixed-rate mortgages and the building of more new houses.

THE EURO? WHAT'S THAT?

Following the furor made over the Chancellor's assessment of the Five Tests, I waited curiously to hear what he said in his March 2004 Budget. Well, he didn't say a whole lot really. 'There would be no further assessment of British entry into the single currency this year' was the basic message.

Furthermore, it was announced that, come the 2005 Budget, the Treasury would only decide whether a further in-depth assessment of the Five Tests was needed. It wouldn't actually carry out an assessment in time for the 2005 budget.

These announcements made the prospect of the Labour Government holding a referendum on the euro before the next general election very unlikely.

The earliest revised date for a referendum on the euro was suggested as spring 2008 …

EUROCREEP

This delightful phrase refers to the fact that many British businesses already have to accommodate the euro, because they have suppliers or customers in the eurozone. Therefore, costs are already being incurred by many businesses, and will continue to be incurred regardless of whether the UK joins the single currency. Most large British retailers accept euros and most British banks now offer financial products in euro denominations.

THE MONEY

There are eight different Euro notes:
in denominations €5, 10, 20, 50, 100, 200 & 500.

There are 100 cents in a Euro.

There are eight different Euro coins:
in denominations of 1, 2, 5, 10, 20 and 50 cents.

The €500 note was quickly renamed The Gangster's Note, due to its high denomination and likely appeal to money launders and other criminals.

THE DESIGN

The notes are uniform throughout all member states. The coins include a motif particular to each member state on one face only. All coins and notes are redeemable throughout the eurozone. The design of the Euro notes incorporates windows and gateways on one side – as a symbol of *'the spirit of openness and cooperation in the EU.'* The reverse side includes bridges, a metaphor for *'communication between the people of Europe and between Europe and the rest of the world.'*

(The images are all imaginary – a means of avoiding a political scrap over the choice of real windows, gateways and bridges for the designs.)

BUSINESS BENEFITS

The single currency offers three key benefits to businesses:

▸ Lower cash management costs:
   When UK companies operate in eurozone countries, the costs associated with currency conversions will be eliminated.

▸ Reduced Currency Risk:
   Uncertainty over what currency fluctuations might do to the values of orders or contracts, will be eliminated (this is called *hedging*).

▸ A Bigger, More Integrated Market:
   Consumers will be more tempted to purchase across national boundaries (note also the impact of the Internet in tempting 'cross border purchases').

COSTS & SAVINGS

The European Commission has estimated that the euro's total savings for businesses will amount to approx. 0.33 % of total economic output for the whole continent. – About £20 billion a year. Meanwhile, the British Retail Consortium has estimated that the introduction of the euro will cost its members £3.5 billion. The cost will derive from new cashpoints, tills, vending machines, accounting systems, and pricing systems, for example, as well as staff training. The Federation of Small Businesses has estimated the introduction of the euro will cost most of its members approx. £5000 each.

SMALL BUSINESS VIEW

The Federation of Small Businesses has publicly opposed the euro. Only 15% of all UK companies do any trade with the euro area. Almost 80% of small businesses do all their business within a 50-mile radius of their business premises.

THE EURO PREPARATIONS UNIT

Tills, cash dispensers, vending machines, parking meters, and dual currency deposits for supermarket trolleys … there's a lot more to prepare than new pricing and accounting sytems!

The Treasury's **Euro Preparations Unit** has set up 12 Regional Euro Forums to help businesses prepare (even though it seems we may not join the single currency for a while yet). The Euro Preparations Unit is responsible for the National Changeover Plan – which aims to ensure the UK and its relevant systems are in a position to readily adopt the euro, should we ever decide to join the single currency. (Indeed various government departments have already spent millions of pounds on planning and preparations).

It has also launched the 3es Initiative (promoting the combined advantages of e-commerce, the euro and exports). And, it has a web-site … see www.euro.gov.uk.

THE EURO VERSUS THE $US

When the euro was launched on January 1st 1999 it was worth US$1.18.

In late 2000 it dropped to its low, to date, of US$0.82.

In February 2004 it reached its high, to date, of US$1.28.

(Exchange rate graphs are available daily in The Financial Times, if you need current rates. Or, if you want more detailed information, the European Central Bank has some easy-to-read summary graphs, of numerous euro exchange rates, on www.ecb.int.)

TEETHING PROBLEMS!

Between May 1999 and April 2000 the ECB increased interest rates seven times, from 2.5% to 4.75%, in an attempt to restore the euro's value.

In an historic move, both the US Federal Reserve and the Bank of England used millions of pounds worth of reserves to buy the euro, in a valiant attempt to prop it up.

SOME BACKGROUND INFO.

Right. Before we start discussing the debate surrounding the European Union's proposed Constitutional Treaty, I want to touch on the related issue of federalism. Federalism is a key issue in the constitution debate. It means:

Federalism, 1. *n*. the forming of a government in which power is divided between one central and several regional governments

Federation, 1. *n*. the union of several provinces or states. **2.** any alliance or association of organisations which have freely joined together for a common purpose. [*Collins Concise Dictionary*]

Currently, the European Union is not a federation. It is a *treaty-based grouping of sovereign countries*. That means, all member states of the European Union retain political powers of self-governance. Member states must agree to transfer any of their decision-making powers to the European Union.

Sovereignty means *the political power a nation has to govern itself.*

There are many examples of countries that share a united sovereignty but still have individual powers of self-governance over some things (and retain distinct national identities).

The devolution of power to Scotland and Wales, which remains a part of The United Kingdom, is one example.

"THE TALE OF MONNET"

A Frenchman, Jean Monnet, an avid 'Federalist,' played an astonishingly relentless role in the development of the European Union that we have today. What follows is a rather lengthy digression, but a worthy one I think … In the 1920s Monnet and a fellow 'visionary' - Arthur Salter, an English civil servant - were influential figures in The League of Nations (the international agency that in 1945 evolved into The United Nations). They discussed the idea of creating a new form of government in Europe, which was above and beyond the control of national governments. (Such an entity was called a 'Supranational Government.') In 1931 Salter published a collection of papers called *'The United States of Europe.'* Whilst Salter went off to become a Professor of Politics at Oxford, Monnet set about achieving his ambitions.

In 1940 Monnet met with General Charles de Gaulle of France. They discussed the idea of a Franco-British Union, which would include joint armed forces, common citizenship and a common currency. The idea was then discussed with the Head of the UK Foreign Office, who put the plan to Prime Minister Churchill, who liked the idea. The draft text of the Anglo-French Union originated from Monnet (with Salter's assistance.) Churchill struck out references to a common currency, but otherwise supported the draft. However, the French Government rejected the proposal.

Next, in the aftermath of the war, Monnet contributed to the negotiations of The Marshall Plan (the US post-war funding package). In reponse to The Marshall Plan, 16 European nations formed the Organisation for European Economic Co-operation in 1947. Monnet became its Vice-Chairman. In 1950 Monnet wrote a memorandum proposing the integration of Europe's coal and steel industries. The French Government wanted to exercise control over Germany's coal and steel economy, but West Germany, Britain and the US opposed the idea. Fed up, the US Secretary of State called a meeting of Foreign Ministers and demanded the French think of an alternative solution.

Monnet spotted an opportunity and gave his memorandum to the French Foreign Minister, Robert Schuman. Prime Minister Atlee was skeptical of the French proposal to surrender UK sovereignty to a new level of European authority. Monnet insisted the UK make up its mind and imposed a quick deadline (June 2nd 1950.) Atlee was out of London, so the acting-Prime Minister was tracked down and asked for a response. He said the now infamous line ...'The Durham miners won't wear it!' Hence the UK did not participate in the eventual European Coal & Steel Community. Monnet then convinced the French Government that he should represent France in the formal negotiations, even though he wasn't a member of the French Government! Monnet in fact chaired the negotiations, and prepared the draft text proposing the European Coal & Steel Community. In the draft text he wrote comments such as: 'it [the Community] is laying the foundations of a European federation.' (The eventual European Coal & Steel Community replicated the structures suggested by Salter in his 1931 papers on *The United States of Europe.*)

Next, Monnet set about preparing a proposal for a European Defence Community, which required further political integration. His proposal was rejected, so Monnet resigned as President of the European Coal & Steel Community. In 1955, Monnet revised his plans for a European Defence Community, and proposed something that was to become the European Atomic Energy Community (Euratom). He also mooted the idea of a customs market and a common economic market. He liased with the Belgian Foreign Minister, starting the discussions that eventually led to the Treaties of Rome, and the formation of the European Economic Community. Not finished yet, Monnet succeeded in lobbying the Americans and having the Organisation for European Economic Co-operation (OEEC) changed. The OEEC was chaired by the British, and was seen as embodying the British concept of European unity. It was replaced by the Organisation for Economic Co-operation and Development (OECD) in 1961. Monnet died in 1979, aged 90. In 1988, on the centenary of his birth, President Mitterand transferred his ashes to the Pantheon in Paris.

"THE TALE OF SPINELLI"

Another person who pursued a dream of a 'United Federal Europe,' was an Italian Communist called Alberto Spinelli, who spent twelve years in a Fascist prison. During this time he broke with Communism and embraced the idea of a United Europe. He wrote a Manifesto which discussed federalism, entitled 'Towards A Free and United Europe.' It was smuggled to The Italian Resistance in 1941, and lead to a major 'European Federalist Movement' conference being held in Geneva in 1944. The conference declared that, due to a lack of unity on the continent, a single Federal Organisation to govern Europe wouldn't be accepted. Instead, a federal 'Union' was proposed, to provide a 'supranational' tier of government above the individual sovereignty of individual countries.

Many decades later, in 1979, Spinelli (aged 72!) stood as an Independent Member of the European Parliament (MEP). He argued for the total reform of the Treaty of Rome, and formed a cross-party group open to all MEPs, which would promote further European Integration. The group was called the 'Crocodile Club.' Spinelli also launched a semi-official publication called *The Crocodile* (which still exists).

Spinelli's ultimate aim was to get a parliamentary resolution passed, so that a constitutional working group could suggest modifications to the Treaty of Rome. He got his resolution in 1981. His Committee for Institutional Affairs was established in 1982, and its task agreed in 1983 - to transform the 'Community' into a 'European Union.' Spinelli died in 1986, aged 80, but his 'dream' became a reality several years later, on the signing of The Maastricht Treaty.

(NB. It is no coincidence that Spinelli remained on the sidelines until after Monnet's death. Although Monnet apparently respected him, he disliked him.)

CHURCHILL

Churchill took a varied view of federalism. 1n 1942 he said the following: *"I look forward to a United States of Europe in which the barriers between the nations will be greatly minimised and unrestricted travel will be possible. I hope to see the economy of Europe studied as a whole."*

After losing the 1945 General Election, he went on a speaking tour of the USA and Europe, promoting the virtues of political integration in Europe. In 1948 he presided over a Congress of Europe (see below). However, in 1957, when he was re-elected as Prime Minister, Churchill was less enthusiastic about the nature of 'European Integration' being proposed.

THE CONGRESS OF EUROPE

The Congress of Europe was at The Hague in 1948. Over 750 people attended. A resolution of the Congress established The Council of Europe – a consultative assembly of national parliaments, with an aim of *furthering political and economic integration in Europe*. It was an ambitious forum, but was ultimately impotent in its desire to create change due to continuing debate between federalist and anti-federalist members. However, it remains an active forum today. Its main achievement has been the establishment of the Court of Human Rights, which is now an Agency of the European Union.

AMERICA'S ROLE

After the Hague Congress, campaigners for European integration went to America to lobby for support, and met the founder of the CIA, amongst other people. Following the erection of the Berlin Wall, America was dead keen on the idea of a United Europe. (*Allegedly*, the CIA contributed millions of dollars of covert funding to the Council of Europe to keep the idea afloat.)

In 1949 a Statute of the Council was signed by ten governments, which formed a Committee of Ministers and a Consultative Assembly. However, debate over the Council's federal intentions continued. By 1951 little progress had been made, and the Council accepted its limited role as a 'talking shop.'

DID FEDERALISM CATCH ON?

Some people argue that the European Union's guiding principle of 'Subsidiarity' is for all intents and purposes federalism, merely called a different name. Others say that subsidiarity is quite a different thing.

'Subsidiarity' requires decisions to be taken at the lowest possible level of government to the citizens. In other words, the EU will only take action when its objectives can't be adequately met by member states acting individually, or when it's believed that an objective will be better achieved by member states acting in common.

IS FEDERALISM REALLY SO BAD?

Federalism aims to create *diversity* through autonomous tiers of local government that can respond to local issues and cultures. As a political system it is meant to combine the advantages of small states (the local tiers of government) with the advantages of large states (the central tier).

A federalist structure is also meant to offer security, by working against the creation of excessive central power or the domination of one member government over another.

The catch, in the European Union's case, is that once a power (or 'competence') has been passed from a local government tier (member state governments) to the 'central tier' (the EU), it can't be returned unless *it is agreed unanimously by all member states.*

This principle is called *acquis communautaire.*

The European Union's definitive 'Book of Rules' is called the *Acquis Communautaire*. It is over 80,000 pages long!

CURRENT CONCERNS

I have unearthed four key arguments surrounding the issue of federalism and the European Union today:

▸ That the Economic and Monetary Union (EMU) will inevitably lead to *political union*. Such political union might take the shape of a federation, and this would be a bad thing.

▸ That EMU will not/should not lead to a full political union, and the threat of full *political integration* is just a scare-tactic being used by the anti-euro lobby, who don't want *economic integration*.

▸ That there's nothing wrong or scary with the notion of a 'Federal Europe.' However, because EMU is so riddled with faults, the single currency will cause political *disintegration* rather than integration, which would be a bad thing.

▸ That the concept and aims of federalism are horrendously misunderstood and misrepresented, and someone should sort out the public's ignorance on the matter!

MORE ABOUT SOVEREIGNTY

Opponents of both the single currency and the new Constitution for Europe refer to a potential loss of sovereignty as a bad thing. They raise the following points:

▸ The loss of self-government in regard to the daily running of our nation should be avoided.

▸ They fear advances in political union will diminish our sovereignty to the extent that we have little self-governance left at all.

▸ They fear a loss of nationalist pride, identity and culture. (Though others argue that identity and culture aren't affected by federalist structures. In the USA, for example, everyone is an American at one level, but a New Yorker, a Texan, or a Californian, at another level. - Can we be British *and* European?)

Some other things people say about sovereignty:

▸ Further political and economic integration will mean the UK will only 'pool' its sovereignty rather than lose it outright.

▸ As a member of the EU, the UK Government regularly 'pools sovereignty' at European Council meetings, in the interests of achieving European Union objectives.

IN FAVOUR OF POLITICAL UNION

Federalism, and the increased political union it stands for, is supported by many. For example, the German Bundesbank has issued two separate statements stressing that *monetary union* will only be durable if accompanied by *political union*. Wim Dusineberg (the former European Central Bank President) has said the process of monetary union must go hand in hand with political integration. And during an interview with CNN (January 2002), the European Commission President, Romani Prodi, said of the euro:

'It is a completely political step ... the historical significance of the euro is to construct a bipolar economy in the world. The two poles are the dollar and the euro. That is the political meaning of the single European currency. It is a step beyond which there will be others. The euro is just an antipasto.'

CONCERNS

Some people believe increased political integration would:
- be unwieldy and *simply wouldn't work*
- have even more layers of horrendous bureaucracy
  (It currently takes an average of two years for a proposal to get agreement by all EU Institutions, and a further two years for the agreement to be implemented as national law)
- impose crippling regulations on businesses
- dissolve the individuality and identity of European countries
- require *relentless and continuous political will* from all member states, which isn't always achieved easily.

EXAMPLES OF FEDERATIONS

Reference is frequently made to the United States of America. There seems to be a common assumption that the USA is the 'best' or only model of federalism, and therefore a more politically integrated Europe would replicate it exactly. There are in fact numerous examples of federations, which differ in a variety of ways from the United States. Ironically perhaps, the British Empire founded many of them as it conquered the world: Australia, India and Canada for example.

The critical difference in models of federalism is the degree of power 'handed over' to the central tier of government, and how much power and influence is retained by the 'nation state unit.'

A NEW CONSTITUTION

Amidst the debates about federalism that were taking place at the time, in December 2000 the European Council made an important announcement regarding the future structure of the European Union. An 'Intergovernmental Conference' would *define how power will be divided between the European Union and national Governments.*

In essence, it was announced that the European Union would have a new Constitution.

PERFECT TIMING

In March 1999, The 20 Commissioners of the European Commission, lead by Jacques Santer, resigned after a damning report accused them of fraud, nepotism and mismanagement! (Ooops!) The new Commissioners, led by Romano Prodi, are still, allegedly, clawing back influence and reputation after the scale of the fiasco.

The point of this in regard to federalism is the question, just what is the 'centre' of the European Union?

The European Commission is less powerful than it was, whereas representatives of the 'nation state unit' (the European Council) are forming powerful alliances through new methods of decision making. However, the 5th Enlargement has made these alliances (or 'axis of power' as they're sometimes referred to) more complex and changeable. (Because alliances between member states change depending on the specific issue being debated.)

Therefore it is now seen to be a very opportune time to write a constitution that reviews and outlines:

▸ *how* power is divided both within the European Union, and between the European Union and member states,
▸ and, *how* decisions are made.

CONVENTION ON THE FUTURE OF EUROPE

During 2002/2003 a seventeen month Convention on The Future of Europe was chaired by former French President, Valery Giscard d'Estaing. The Convention had 105 members and a 13 member 'Praesidium.'

The Convention conducted three distinct phases: a 'listening phase,' a 'deliberating phase,' and 'proposing phase.' In May 2003 the Convention presented its Draft Constitution. The 16 draft articles covered:

Articles 1-4:   The definition, objectives and values of the European Union

Articles 5-7:   The fundamental rights and citizenship of the European Union

Articles 8-16: The European Union's powers, and division of policy responsibilities between European Union institutions and Member States.

The Draft Constitution brings together the existing European Union treaties into a single legal text. Summary documents and transcripts from The Convention are available on the EU's server, http://europa.eu.int.

WHAT THE CONVENTION DID

No matter what you may think of its content, you need to stop for a second and be impressed by the sheer industriousness of the Draft Constitution process. The Convention Members:

▸ heard over '1800 interventions' during plenary sessions

▸ established 11 Working Parties and 3 Discussion Circles

▸ received 1264 contributions from National Government Organisations and the business and academic communities

▸ had specific meetings with relevant groups, such as churches

▸ held a Youth Convention.

They then put all documents on the Convention's official website (in all the national languages no less.) The website had over 47,000 hits a month, rising to 100,000 per month in the closing months.

Alas, I suspect that too few of these website hits originated from the UK, but that's not entirely The Convention's fault is it?

WHAT THE CONSTITUTION PROPOSES

▸ The creation of an EU Foreign Minister, who will promote a common European Union foreign policy.

▸ The Charter of Fundamental Human Rights will become legally binding (the Charter was adopted by the EU in 2000 but currently is not legally binding). The UK is arguing that it mustn't extend the European Court of Justice's judicial reach into domestic labour and social policy.

▸ To merge the EU's existing three treaties into one. The European Union will - for the first time - become a legal entity in its own right (instead of being a treaty-based grouping of sovereign countries.)

▸ To provide - for the first time - a mechanism by which a member state could leave the European Union.

▸ To extend 'Qualified Majority Voting' to circa. 20 areas previously protected by the Unanimous Voting process, which would mean member states would lose their right to exercise their national Veto.

▸ The European Parliament will gain new powers in 36 areas, including the ability to legislate in areas such as justice and home affairs, and the right to have a say over big budget items, such as the Common Agricultural Policy and EU Structural Funds.

▸ A European Public Prosecution Office.

MORE PROPOSALS

▶ The European Commission to be reduced in size to 15 Commissioners, after 2009. All member states will take equal turns in sitting on the Commission.

▶ New methods of decision making; including:
A Double Majority in the Council of Ministers. (In which half of member states comprising 60% of the population must agree to pass a decision. This would replace the voting rights agreed, after immense debate, in 2000.)
'Co-decisions' between the European Parliament (representing the people) and the European Council (representing the member states). If a third of member state national parliaments reject any proposal, the European Commission would have to 'reconsider' it.

▶ A full-time President will chair the European Council. The President will serve for two and a half years, renewable once. This will replace the existing six-month rotating presidency of the European Council by member states. The exact details of the role remain ambiguous.

▶ A new 'Bridging Clause' would allow member states to abolish national vetoes in the future, if they agree to do so unanimously. (Currently, this can only be achieved via a treaty change.)

▶ A new legal concept: member states will be bound by an 'obligation of loyal cooperation' which means that the first duty of national governments should be to the European Union.

THE OFFICIAL QUOTE

In July 2003 the Convention President presented 'The Rome Declaration' to the Italian Presidency of the European Council (it rotates every six months, remember.) Mr Giscard Estaing's declaration said (amongst lots of other things):

"With this Constitution, Europe is taking a decisive step towards political union: a union of citizens and a union of Member States. The Constitution:

▶ enshrines citizens' rights by incorporating the European Charter of Fundamental Rights;

▶ turns Europe towards its citizens by holding out new opportunities for them to participate;

▶ establishes a clear, transparent apportionment of powers between the union and its Member States, enabling national parliaments to intervene. The Union's powers are extended in areas where that is what citizens want;

▶ provides Europe with stable, democratic and effective institutions:

- the <u>European Parliament</u> becomes the Union's main legislature. It will enact laws together with the Council. European legislation will be the product of agreement between citizens' elected representatives and States;

- the <u>Council</u> will have a face and a measure of durability; its President will organise States' work and will be able to plan for the future and think ahead;

- the <u>Commission</u>, organised so as to fulfill its European role, will act as a driving force and the main executive. It will embody the common European interest."

REACTION TO THE DRAFT CONSTITUTION

I'm sure you won't be surprised to hear that reaction to the draft Constitution was both loud and varied! The backbone of the Constitution is - by necessity I suppose - compromise. Every member state had to horse-trade items on its wish list, and consequently each member state had a different list of things they liked and disliked about the draft document.

Some critics suggested it focused too much on how powers should be divided between the European Union and member states, and not enough on how these powers should be *democratically controlled.*

Some critics said it was just too long and too ambiguous.

Some critics said it went too far: that it was reversing the European Union's underlying principle of Subsidiarity and robbing member states of too many domestic decision-making powers. (Some critics noted that every proposed change in decision-making involved transferring power from member state governments to the European Union.)

Others said it didn't go far enough to cement the political union that Europe desperately needs. (And this will make you laugh: because of the controversy surrounding it, the word 'Federation' was removed from the document altogether!)

THE ALTERNATIVE PLAN

Eight members of The Convention on the Future of Europe did not endorse the Draft Constitution. They tabled an alternative report to the European Council, called 'Laeken's Lost Missions.' They argued that the Draft Constitution did not meet the requirements of the Laeken Declaration of December 2001 (in which the Convention for the Future of Europe process was announced). The alternative report makes some quite hefty accusations about the Draft Convention process: that Valery Giscard d'Estaing did not allow democracy and normal voting to take place, for example. It is on http://europa.eu.int if you'd like to read it.

THE WHITE PAPER

In September 2003 the UK Government published a White Paper on the Draft Constitution. It established some 'red lines' - the things that the UK Government would not be willing to compromise on during on-going negotiations. The 'red lines' were the retaining of Unanimous Voting (i.e. the right to veto) for decision-making relating to:

▶   all treaty changes
▶   tax, social security, defence and border controls
▶   key areas of criminal procedural law
▶   the EU's 'own resources' revenue-raising mechanisms (i.e. the setting of member state contributions).

MEANWHILE, BACK HOME IN THE NATIONAL PRESS

The UK press was having a fine old time!

The *Sun* ran a headline 'Blair Surrenders Britain to Europe.' The *Daily Mail* ran with 'A Blueprint for Tyranny.' *The Telegraph* even published an article by some chap called Gordon Brown, who said 'Flexibility, not Federalism is Key to this Competitive New World.'

Meanwhile the politicians were being lambasted for trying to belittle the importance of the draft Constitution. 'It's just a bit of housekeeping, tidying up existing treaties,' they said.

The British public started to make noises. Let us have a say! Hold a referendum! But Tony Blair said there was no need, Parliament will make the decision. (There wasn't a referendum on The Maastricht Treaty, remember.)

Jack Straw, Foreign Secretary, reassured us by saying things like, 'nation states must remain the primary source of political legitimacy in Europe.'

And Tony Blair reminded us of the 'red lines' he had drawn: representing the things he wouldn't compromise on during constitution negotiations (i.e. we needn't worry).

THE DAILY MAIL NATIONAL REFERENDUM BALLOT

In June 2003 The Daily Mail newspaper held a National Referendum ballot. They recruited thousands of corner shops and newsagents across the country, who provided voting slips and ballot boxes. The public could also vote by telephone, mobile phone text, or email. The question put to the public was:

> *A new EU constitution is being negotiated and MPS will decide whether the UK accepts it. Do you think the final decision should be put to a referendum of the British people? Yes, or No.*

Over 1.6 million votes were received. 89.88% of voters said Yes, they do want a referendum on the new EU constitution.

PUBLIC OPINION

Whilst the UK media fueled its own frenzy, the EU statisticians, Eurobarometer*, did a survey. Only 39% of Europeans knew what The Convention on the Future of Europe even did. Although the lengthy process of writing a draft constitution was meant to have embraced and involved the European public, it appeared to have been largely ignored by many European citizens. Unfortunately - as a Spanish member of the Convention admitted - 'It is hardly the type of reading you pick up at an airport.'
* survey undertaken in June 2003.

THE CONSTITUTION TIMETABLE

In his Rome Declaration Mr Giscard d'Estaing called on the Italian Presidency to conduct an 'Intergovernmental Conference' at the highest political level, so as to complete matters by December 2003. (Intergovernmental Conferences - IGCS - are required whenever changes to EU Treaties are discussed. This IGC was tasked with turning the Draft Constitution into a new treaty, which would require the agreement of all member states.) The Brussels Summit was held in December 2003, but the complex negotiations surrounding the Draft Constitution weren't completed. The official press release said: ' … it was not possible for the Intergovernmental Conference to reach an overall agreement on a draft constitutional treaty at this stage.'

WHO DUG THEIR HEALS IN?

The December 2003 negotiations broke down after Poland and Spain refused to give up the favourable European Council voting rights they secured in 2000. The new constitution proposed a 'Double Majority' method of decision making, which would result in Spain and Poland having less clout. After a new Spanish Government was elected in 2004, their new Prime Minister agreed to compromise. Then Poland eventually agreed to compromise after the German Chancellor had a wee chat with their Prime Minister.

THE BRUSSELS SUMMIT

Spain and Poland's readiness to compromise meant the European Council could re-open negotiations on the Constitutional Treaty in March 2004. Member state leaders committed themselves to a new deadline: that the IGC must be brought to a conclusion by June 2004. The Irish President of the European Council, Bertie Ahern, said, 'There is a strong will to find a way forward and I think that everyone understands that there will have to be compromise.' Mr Ahern noted three key issues that continued to cause problems for the delegation:

▶ The size and composition of the European Commission
▶ The definition and scope of Qualified Majority Voting
▶ The number of seats per member state in the European Parliament.

The new push to finalise the Constitutional Treaty set the UK media all aflutter. Would Tony Blair's 'red lines' be safe? (As Jack Straw confessed, 'Nothing is agreed until everything is agreed.')

There was concern in the UK that the new timetable - to have the new Constitutional Treaty agreed by June 2004 - smacked of a fast-track 'let's get this thing sorted as quick as we can' approach. (Though few people believed that the ambitious deadline of June 2004 would be met anyway.)

A MOST DRAMATIC U-TURN!

In April 2004, something quite historic happened!

(In fact it may be the only reason many of you bothered to buy this book?)

Prime Minister Tony Blair announced that, despite all sorts of previous statements to the contrary, he would offer us a referendum on the proposed Constitutional Treaty after all!

The Prime Minister acknowledged that the referendum vote would be about the Constitutional Treaty, but would have much wider implications.

This is an extract from the Prime Minister's Common's speech:
'It is time to resolve once and for all whether this country, Britain, wants to be at the centre and heart of European decision-making or not; time to decide whether our destiny lies as a leading partner and ally of Europe or on the margins. …Let the issue be put. Let the battle be joined.'

Well of course, all sorts of political shenanigans burst forth.

Why Mr Blair's sudden change of heart?

BLAIR'S REASONS?

The following reasons for the Prime Minister's announcement were suggested in the media:

▶ Announcing an UK referendum might boost Mr Blair's negotiating position with other member state leaders over the final wording of the Constitutional Treaty. (Which would help to protect the UK's 'red lines.')

▶ The announcement would deprive the Tories of a key campaigning theme for the June 2004 European Parliament elections, and the UK 2005 general elections.

▶ Mr Blair was fearful that rebels in the Commons and/or Lords could force an amendment in the Government's Constitution Bill, insisting on a referendum anyway.

▶ By delaying the UK referendum for as long as possible, other member states might return a referendum No vote before us.

▶ There was some speculation that pressure from one newspaper group especially - in the form of, 'hold a referendum or we won't support Labour in the next general election' - helped Mr Blair to change his mind. (I have no idea whether or not this was the case. You can make your own minds up!)

WHEN TO HOLD IT?

The Prime Minister made it clear that a referendum would not be held until after the 2005 general elections. The Tories demanded that it should be held sooner. At the time of writing, the process that must be followed is this:

June 2004: Constitutional Treaty final wording agreed by EU leaders*

November 2004: European Commission lawyers finish drawing up and translating Treaty document, ready for ratification.

2004/2005: The UK Government would introduce a Constitution Bill (or similar such name) to Parliament. (Mr Blair wants Parliament to ratify the Constitutional Treaty before the public referendum.)

2005: An Act of Parliament is required for the staging of a referendum. The Act would set out details of how and when the vote would be held.

2005: Ten weeks is required to pass between the passing of the Act of Parliament and the actual day of the referendum.

*If the European Council doesn't finalise the Constitutional Treaty in June 2004, the process will be delayed, by a further six months minimum. (You can check off what has happened, at the time you are reading this book, by using the summary chart on page 125, or by visiting www.hot-potato.info.)

REFERENDUMS EVERYWHERE?

The following member states have so far confirmed they will 'most probably' ratify the new Constitutional Treaty via a referendum: Spain, Portugal, the Netherlands (where it will be the first in the country's history), Luxembourg, Ireland, Denmark, Estonia, and the Czech Republic.

Germany - ironically - has a constitution that prohibits referendums, so they won't be having one.

Italy has said they won't be having one.

President Chirac promised the French they would have one, but at the time of writing has yet to confirm this.

If any member states receives a 'No' vote in their referendum, the constitution becomes null and void. If this happens in a small member state, they may be pushed to hold a second referendum.

If, however, one of the larger member states - the UK or France, say - returns a No vote, it is likely the details of the constitution will need to be renegotiated.

Member states will have two years to ratify the Constitutional Treaty.

REFERENDUM FACTS

The recognised 'Yes' and 'No' campaigning organisations for the referendum will be able to spend up to £5 million each on advertising in the run up to the referendum. Each camp will receive £600,000 of taxpayer's money. Other, informal campaigning groups can spend a maximum of £500,000 each on advertising, but will not receive any public money. The Government will propose the wording for the referendum's question, but the independent Electoral Commission will scrutinise the wording and change it if this is deemed necessary.

THE EUROPEAN PARLIAMENT ELECTIONS

There are 732 elected Members of the European Parliament (MEPs), 78 of them from the UK. Mainstream television adverts encouraged us to take part in the June 2004 elections, as in the 1999 elections turnout in the UK was the lowest of any EU member state. Only 24% of the electorate bothered to show up. (In comparison, in the 2001 UK general elections voter turnout was 59%.) It was hoped that the constitution debate might increase voter interest (and turnout) in the June 2004 European Parliament elections.

(By the way, in Belgium, Greece and Luxembourg voting is compulsory.)

SOME FINAL COMMENTS

▶ We should not assume that the Constitutional Treaty will ever be agreed, until it is agreed.

▶ We should not assume a referendum on the Constitutional Treaty will be held in the UK, until it is held. (A No vote in another member state's referendum may scupper the process before ours takes place.)

▶ Oh yes. And I need to dispel an urban myth that's going around … If the UK returns a No vote in the referendum on the Constitutional Treaty, it does not mean we'll be 'booted out' of Europe.

▶ In fact, the Constitutional Treaty, for the first time, will allow a member state to withdraw from the European Union altogether.

WHAT THE PEOPLE THOUGHT

In February 2004 *Eurobarometer* (the European Union public opinion monitor) released some results on the draft Constitution. The polls included the countries about to join the EU in the 5th Enlargement.

▸ 77% of citizens agreed the EU must adopt a Constitution.

▸ Only Sweden (58%) and the UK (51%) scored support of less than 60% for the Draft Constitution.

▸ 67% of citizens felt the work of the EU institutions may be blocked in the absence of a Constitution.

▸ Three-quarters of citizens did not feel well informed about the Draft Constitution.

General *Eurobarometer* polls are undertaken twice a year. The latest poll results (Spring 2004, EU15 only) are:

▸ **Is membership of the EU a good thing?**
EU15 average: 48% yes
UK: 29% yes - lowest in EU

▸ **Do you receive any benefit from the EU?**
EU15 average: 47% yes
UK: 30% yes - 2nd lowest in EU (Sweden @ 27%)

▸ **Do you support the single currency?**
EU15 average: 60% yes
UK: 26% yes - lowest in EU

▸ **Do you support Enlargement of the EU?**
EU15 average: 52% yes
UK: 31% yes - 2nd lowest in EU (Germany @ 28%)

▸ **Do you trust the European Commission?**
EU15 average: 47% yes
UK: 26% - lowest in EU

THE EUROPEAN COMMISSION

The three broad objectives of the European Commission are:

▶ to initiate proposals for new legislation
▶ to act as 'guardian' of the European Union's treaties
▶ to act as manager and executor of European Union policies and international agreements (e.g. trade relationships).

The European Commission's roles and responsibilities mean it is at 'the heart' of European Union decision making.

From November 2004 there will be 25 Commissioners (the Draft Constitution proposes the number be reduced to 15.)

The Commissioners, supported by thousands of staff members, propose 'draft directives' - which must be approved by the European Council and the European Parliament. The Commissioners provide both political leadership and direction. They are obliged to be completely independent of their national governments, and are appointed for five-year terms.

The European Commission is divided into 25 directorates-general (DGs). Each is headed by a director-general (who in turn reports to a specific Commissioner). The directorates-general are responsible for carrying out research and consultation relating to proposals for new directives. They are also responsible for monitoring existing legislation, and ensuring that member states comply.

DO YOU BELIEVE EVERYTHING YOU READ IN THE PRESS?

As a quick aside, I simply have to share the following little gem I uncovered. The following are all stories that have been printed in the British press:

▶   'EU to force fisherman to wear hairnets on boats!'
▶   'EU ban sale of home-made jams and cakes at village fetes!'
▶   'EU to ban round gin bottles, which must now be square!'
▶   'EU demands Christmas trees are symmetrical, with regularly spaced needles!'
▶   'EU to ban prawn cocktail flavoured crisps!'
▶   'EU says eggs will have to be stamped with details of the hen that laid them.'
▶   'EU to rename Waterloo Station 'Europe Station' [so as not to upset the French]
▶   'EU Regulations mean the end of bendy bananas and curved cucumbers.'
▶   'Corgis to be banned by the EU.'
▶   'British ambulances to be repainted yellow - for Europe.'

Every one of these headlines is untrue and distorts any story that existed behind it. So commonplace is such reporting, the European Union operate a dedicated 'Euromyth' press service in an attempt to clarify the facts from the histrionics.

DO WE NEED TO BE PART OF EUROPE?'

This issue is raised frequently in both the single currency and the Constitution for Europe debate. It has both economic and political considerations.

Those who argue the UK does need to be allied to Europe suggest that in today's modern world the UK is too small to 'go it alone.' To survive and prosper we must be allied to a larger trading bloc, and benefit from both the external influence and power that a trading bloc offers.

OR DON'T WE?

Those who argue that the UK doesn't need to be allied to Europe inform us that the UK is the fourth largest economy in the world, and that actually - for a little island – it does very well.

It is also argued that, even if the UK keeps sterling and doesn't join the single currency in the foreseeable future, we will still (we assume!) remain a member state of the European Union, and thus will benefit from all the other benefits of membership, including the Single Market.

THE REST OF THE WORLD

Then there's the argument that the UK would be wrong to put all its economic eggs in just one basket - that is, an economic alliance with Europe.

Supporters of this argument say the single currency will bring a) instability and b) over-regulated economies, which will risk the UK's competitive edge against the dynamic markets in other parts of the world, such as the USA and the Pacific Rim.

BE LEADERS, NOT FOLLOWERS

Supporters of the single currency argue that Europe should be a leader in world market trends, not a follower.

A Single Market (and this is what the EU has been working towards for decades, remember) simply *won't work* without a single currency. Without a single currency, Europe's economies will remain divided and weak, they say.

And with divided and weak economies, Europe won't be able to exercise *global influence and leadership.*

UK TRADE: SOME FACTS

The UK exports more to the EU than we import from the EU.

But the UK imports more from the rest of the world than we export to the rest of the world.

Therefore, the sterling currency fluctuations are advantageous for some businesses and disadvantageous to others: it depends on which countries they export to and import from. Many UK exporters and importers would prefer the security that a fixed exchange rate between the UK and other EU member states would provide.

Some figures:
▸ In 2001, 57.5% of all exported UK goods went to EU countries.

▸ In 2001, 50% of all UK imports came from EU countries.

▸ In comparison, in Luxembourg, Belgium, the Netherlands, Spain and Portugal, over 70% of all exported goods are exported to other European Union member states. (In France the figure is 60.8% and in Germany it is 65.7%.)

[Source: Eurostat]

FOREIGN INVESTMENT

The Press has fuelled much speculation about the potential impact of the UK's euro decision on Japanese investment in the UK. The UK receives almost half of Japanese investment in Europe. Japan is second (behind the USA) in the flow of new projects and jobs into the UK. So, should we be concerned that newspapers have reported that companies such as Sony, Nissan and Toyota have hinted they might reduce or stop manufacturing in the UK should it remain outside of the single currency? Or, do we believe the newspaper that suggests the Japanese are merely using the euro debate as a convenient cover to make some tough decisions on production location? Might decisions to reduce or close manufacturing in the UK actually be fuelled by shifts in demand, obsolete products, and pricing pressures in world markets (e.g. it's cheaper to move factories to Thailand or South Korea)?

Then there are reports that the new member states in Eastern and Central Europe will attract investment away from Western Europe, because of their low labour and business costs.

At least, despite currency fluctuation issues, the UK remains a low-cost location for foreign investment in Western Europe, because of its tax and labour regulation advantages. We also have the advantage of the English language.

E-DAY!

On September 1st 2001 convoys of armoured trucks began the delivery of the 50 billion euro coins (that's 250,000 tons, enough metal to build 24 Eiffel Towers!) and the 14.5 billion euro notes. (If laid end to end, the new notes would stretch to the moon and back twice!) The money was delivered first to banks and businesses across the eurozone in a 'front-loading' phase of E-Day preparations, allowing staff three months for training. Unfortunately, the euro was introduced on January 1st - just in time for the mayhem of New Year sales.

EUROPE DAY

Europe Day marks the anniversary of Robert Schuman's speech, on May 9th 1950, in which the idea of a European Community was first raised. (Would we take more notice of it if it May 9th was declared a Bank Holiday?)

THE FLAG

The European Flag was originally designed in 1955 for The Council of Europe - a separate body from the EU altogether. In 1985 it became the official European emblem. The circle of stars represents solidarity and harmony between the people of Europe. The number of them - twelve - is a symbolic number representing 'perfection, completeness and unity.'

ARE WE BETTER?

The British clearly have a lack of interest in the European Union. Do we assume that the British way of life is best, and that we have nothing to learn or gain from the EU? Consider this:

(Statistics are for EU15 member states. Most are from Eurostat)

▶ Britain loses five times as many workdays from strikes than France.

▶ Our infant mortality rates are higher than the EU average.

▶ We endure the longest working hours of any EU country.

▶ The percentage of our 18 year olds entering higher education is lower than most of Europe.

▶ Despite increased competition, we still pay two-thirds more for our phone calls than the EU average.

▶ Despite having a high employment rate, 17% of UK children live in jobless households - the highest rate in the EU (including the 5th Enlargement countries!)

▶ Of the EU15 member states we are ranked 6th for CO_2 emissions per capita. We have the 4th highest employment rate. We are ranked 11th for the level of government spending on welfare benefits per capita. We are ranked 7th for the % of the population who own a personal computer. We have the 3rd highest population density. We are ranked 7th for our overall standard of living.

▶ We have fewer Bank Holidays than the EU average.

▶ We invest below the EU average per capita in Research and Development.

▶ We have a really, really crap rail network.

AND FINALLY . . .

I would like to respond to the man I once encountered on the London Underground's Circle Line.

With regard to your loud and vociferous lamenting that the single currency will result in British children wearing *lederhosen* to school, I can confirm, I found no reference to this 'fact' during any of my research for this book. Please rest assured.

DISCLAIMER

I have tirelessly checked the accuracy of my information. But, unfortunately, I accept no responsibility if you use this book as your key Thesis reference, or to close a deal, impress the boss, secure a new job, or chat up a member of the opposite sex,* and it all goes horribly wrong when they correct you on a minor point.

* it is not recommended you use the European Union for this purpose.

THE LEGAL BIT

The greatest care has been taken in compiling this book. However, no responsibility can be accepted by the publishers or author for the accuracy of the information presented. Where opinion is expressed it is that of the author.

FURTHER RESOURCES

▸ **The European Union server** is fantastic: http://europa.eu.int. Or, try their official 'EU in America' website, www.eurunion.org.

▸ **The UK Information Offices for the European Parliament:**
2 Queen Anne's Gate, London SW1H 9AA.
Ph 020 7227 4300, email: eplondon@europarl.eu.int.
The Tun, 4 Jackson's Entry, Holyrood Road, Edinburgh EH8 8PJ, Ph. 0131 557 7866,
email epedinburgh@europarl.eu.int.
UK Representation for the European Commission:
www.cec.org.uk.
Jean Monnet House, 8 Storey's Gate, London SW1P 3AT.
Ph. 020 7973 1992.
2 Caspian Point, Caspian Way, Cardiff CF10 4QQ,
Ph. 029 2089 5020.
9 Alva St, Edinburgh EH2 4PH, Ph. 0131 225 2058.
Windsor House, 9/15 Bedford Street, Belfast BT2 7EG.
Ph. 028 9024 0708.

▸ European Central Bank, www.ecb.int.

▸ www.euro.gov.uk (Site of the UK Euro Preparations Unit)

▸ www.europe.gov.uk (Foreign & Commonwealth Office)

▸ My website - I will be providing simple updates of main events as they happen: www.hot-potato.info

▸ If you don't have access to a computer, visit your local Reference Library's European Union information section.

A NOTE ON MY SOURCES

I have spent the past four years avidly reading all flavours of daily newspapers, almost all the EU publications in my local library, and downloading official documents off numerous websites. These basic sources - newspapers, the library and the web - unearthed mountains of information. Indeed, finding the information was easy; making sense of any of it was the hard part. (Even more of a challenge was cross-referencing it, checking it, and editing my folders of collected information into a mere 128 pages!) Because I wanted this to be a simple book for normal people, I have avoided cross-referencing my work with numerous references to academic or specialist books. I have, however, found the following books particularly useful, which I would like to note:

The European Union Handbook, 2nd Ed. (2002), J. Glover (Editor), (Fitzroy Dearborn, London).

The Great Deception: the secret history of the European Union, 2004, C. Booker and R. North, (Continuum, London).
(This book was useful not because of the negative premise it was presenting, but because of the detail it gives of the people, politics and processes behind the development of the European Union.)

The Economist Guide to the European Union, 2002, D. Leonard, (Profile Books, London).

The Penguin Companion to European Union, 2002, T. Bainbridge, (Penguin, London).

GLOSSARY OF KEY TERMS

Charter of Fundamental Rights: established in 2000 by the *European Council*. It contains a comprehensive list of social, political and economic rights that EU citizens should expect the *European Union* to recognize and respect.

Common Agricultural Policy (CAP): the EU's long-standing protectionist policy for agriculture. It has been criticised for years, on both cost and environmental grounds, and has recently been substantially reformed.

Common External Tariff: the customs tariff all EU *member states* apply to goods entering from outside the EU.

Common Market: The popular name used originally for the *European Economic Community*, which was established in 1958. The aims of the common market were to free up movement of goods, labour, services and capital between participating countries, and to establish trade protection for participating countries.

Convergence Criteria: the economic conditions set out in the *Treaty on European Union* (otherwise known as the *Masstricht Treaty*), which *member states* must meet before they are eligible to participate in the *single currency*.

Copenhagen Criteria: the criteria, agreed in 1993, that assess the eligibility of countries for EU membership (covering things like democratic governing institutions, human rights, a functioning market economy, for example).

Economic & Monetary Union (EMU): *The Maastricht Treaty* set out a timetable for achieving the longstanding aim of adopting a *single currency* in all member states, together with a more comprehensive coordination of economic policies.

Enlargement: the term given to the expansion of the European Union to include new member states. There have been five 'enlargements' to date: 1973 (Denmark, Ireland, UK); 1981 (Greece); 1986 (Spain, Portugal); 1995 (Austria, Sweden, Finland), and 2004 (The Czech Republic, Slovakia, Poland, Slovenia, Malta, Hungary, Cyprus, Estonia, Latvia and Lithuania).

EU15: the name given to the 15 *member states* which belonged to the European Union prior to the 2004 enlargement.

Euro: the name of the single currency introduced as a result of the EU's *Economic and Monetary Union process*. Euro notes and coins replaced national currencies, in those *member states* participating in the *single currency*, on January 1st 2002.

European Atomic Energy Community (Euratom): one of three European Communities established in the 1950s. Euratom was established in 1957 to promote research and development in atomic energy and to ensure the peaceful and appropriate use of nuclear energy. In 1965 the *Merger Treaty* established a Single Commission and Single Council for the three existing European Communities.

European Central Bank: an independent body established in 1998, to manage the monetary policy of the *eurozone*, and manage the foreign exchange operations and reserves of those *member states* participating in the *Economic and Monetary Union*. It is based in Frankfurt.

European Coal and Steel Community (ECSC): the first of the three European Communities founded in the 1950s. Established in 1952 under the terms of *The Treaty of Paris*, it aimed to control coal and steel resources, initially so that individual states would be unable to develop a military capacity to wage war. In 1965 the *Merger Treaty* established a Single Commission and Single Council for the three existing European Communities.

European Commission: an institution of the *European Union* that carries out the day-to-day work of the European Union, including the drafting of new laws and directives. The Commissioners are assisted by circa 24,000 civil servants. The President of the Commission is chosen by member state governments and must be approved by the European Parliament.

European Community: created by the Maastricht Treaty, it replaced the *European Economic Community*, and is the collective name of the three European Communities created in the 1950s. It became one of the three areas (or 'pillars') of the *European Union*.

European Council: the most influential of the *European Union's* institutions in which leaders of *member states* take decisions. It was formerly known as The Council of Ministers.

European Court of Human Rights: an agency of the *European Union*, with the responsibility of upholding the Convention on Human Rights. It is based in Strasbourg. It was established by The Council of Europe.

European Court of Justice: the highest court of the *European Union*. Its decisions are enforced through the courts of *member states*. It ensures that relevant laws are applied appropriately, that the Institutions of the *European Union* act lawfully, and that member states fulfill their obligations under the various European Union treaties.

European Economic Area: This was formed in 1994 after complex negotiations between the *European Union* and the *European Free Trade Association* (EFTA) It aimed to extend the European Union's 'single market' across western Europe, and reduce political and economic competition between the two groupings of countries. Many of the EFTA members have since become members of the European Union. Switzerland was the only EFTA member to reject membership of the European Economic area.

European Economic Community (EEC): one of the three European Communities established in the 1950s. The EEC was established via The *Treaty of Rome*, with a key objective of creating a *common market*. In 1965 the *Merger Treaty* established a Single Commission and Single Council for the three existing European Communities.

European Free Trade Association (EFTA): Created in 1960 as an alternative to the *European Economic Community*. It established a free trade area, but did not have the same ambitions for economic or political union. The founding seven members were Austria, Denmark, Norway, Portugal, Sweden, Switzerland and the UK. Iceland and Liechtenstein joined later. In 1994 an agreement between the *European Union* and the EFTA formed the *European Economic Area.*

European Parliament: an institution of the *European Union* composed of publicly elected representatives from each of the member states. There are 732 seats in the European Parliament and elections are held every five years.

European Union (EU): The European Union was created by the *Treaty on European Union*, otherwise known as The *Maastricht Treaty*, which came into force in 1993. The EU comprises three distinct areas, or 'pillars. The first, the European Community (EC) is an evolution of the three original European Communities developed in the 1950s, which were amended in subsequent Treaties. The two other 'pillars' established via the Maastricht Treaty - which are less well known - are the Common Foreign and Security Policy, and Cooperation in Justice and Home Affairs (which has since been renamed Police and Judicial Cooperation in Criminal Matters.) The two latter 'pillars' deal predominantly with Foreign Policy and Criminal Law, and can not issue Directives. Business for the two latter pillars is carried out only in the *European Council*.

Exchange Rate Mechanism (ERM): The European Monetary System was established in 1979 in an attempt to create currency stability between *member states*. The ERM was the mechanism that regulated currency fluctuations, whereby the central banks of member states intervened in international money markets if currency valuations went outside of set limits.

Inter-governmental Conference (IGC): the process by which *member states* negotiate amendments to the *European Union's* treaties. IGC's are undertaken by the *European Council*.

Member States: the name given to countries that belong to the *European Union*.

Own Resources: the term given to the *European Union's* revenue budget. Income is received from four sources: agricultural and sugar duties and levies; customs duties; a proportion of the VAT levied by member states, and a fourth 'resource' based on the GNP (or income) of each member state.

Qualified Majority Voting (QMV): a key method of voting used in the *European Council*, whereby *member states* have a set number of votes allocated, based on their population. Decisions are made when a majority vote is reached. It means decisions can be passed even though an overall consensus hasn't been reached. The number of votes allocated to each member state, and the types of decisions that can be made by QMV, continues to be controversial.

Single currency: the common currency of the *Economic and Monetary Union*, the unit of which is known as the *euro*.

Sovereignty: a political and legal term meaning that the legal authority to make decisions in any state rests with its own national parliament. *Member states* are required to transfer sovereignty, in areas of law and decision making covered in the *European Union's* treaties, to the *European Union*.

Stability & Growth Pact: the rules that members of the *Economic and Monetary Union* must follow, to ensure that those *member states* using the *single currency* implement budgetary discipline, and don't make any economic decisions at a national level that may endanger the strength of the single currency.

Subsidiarity: one of the guiding principles of the *European Union*, whereby decisions must be taken by the lowest (most local) level of government possible, and as close to the citizen as possible.

Supranational: a model of governing collective nations in which individual states participate in a tier of government above their nation state government. They may be forced to accept decisions and outcomes they would not otherwise have chosen. Some people say supranational government represents a <u>loss</u> of national sovereignty, others say it represents a <u>pooling</u> of national sovereignty.

Treaties: a summary of European Union treaties is given on page 7.

Unanimous Voting: a method of decision-making used in the European Council, whereby any member state can block a decision by using their national veto.

THE EURO

1. **Second formal assessment of the Five Tests:**
Happened Yet? ☐ (tick if yes)
Date happened:

2. **Decision to hold a referendum on euro entry announced**
Happened Yet? ☐
Date happened:

3. **Referendum takes place**
(minimum of 4 months required after step 2)
Happened Yet? ☐
Date happened:
Result?

4. **A euro-sterling exchange rate is fixed**
(minimum of 10 months after a referendum)
Happened Yet? ☐
Date happened:
Exchange rate:

5. **Euro notes and coins introduced**
(approximately 20 months after fixing of exchange rate)
Happened Yet? ☐
Date happened:

6. **What I bought with my last pound**

....

THE CONSTITUTION

(tick once happened)

Constitutional Treaty agreed by EU Leaders ☐

Treaty ratified by UK Parliament ☐

UK Referendum - A Yes majority is returned ☐

UK Referendum - A No majority is returned ☐

Treaty ratified by all other member states ☐

Or:
Constitutional Treaty renegotiated
(due to failure of member state referendums) ☐

Member states that returned a No Vote in
their referendums …

Ratification process completed ☐

Constitution comes into force
(date: __/__/__) ☐

See www.hot-potato.info for updates on progress!

QUIZ

1. How many stars are there on the European Union Flag?

2. What is sovereignty?

3. In which decade was The European Union established?

4. In which year were euro notes and coins introduced?

5. Which countries have rejected the single currency in a referendum vote?

6. How many civil servants work for the European Commission?

7. Three European Communities were established in the 1950s. What were they?

8. Which is the smallest member state in the European Union, in terms of size?

9. Which is the largest member state in the European Union, in terms of population?

10. Name three things the European Union's Draft Constitutional Treaty is proposing.

11. In which year did the UK join the European Union?

12. How many countries belong to the European Union?

13. Who is the President of the European Commission?

14. What is the difference between the European Parliament and the European Council?

15. Approximately how much money does the UK contribute to the European Union every year?

ANSWERS: Are all inside this book ...